EXTREME PLANNING FOR AUTHORS:

A TREASURE MAP FOR PLANNING YOUR NOVEL

CHRISTY NICHOLAS, CPA

GREEN DRAGON PUBLISHING

First Edition

Copyright © 2022 Christy Nicholas
Cover art by GetCovers
Internal design © 2022 by Christy Nicholas

All rights reserved. No part of this book may be reproduced in any form or by any electronic or mechanical means including information storage and retrieval systems, except in the case of brief quotations embodied in critical articles or reviews, without permission in writing from its publisher, Green Dragon Publishing.
The characters and events portrayed in this book are fictitious or are used fictitiously. Any similarity to real persons, living or dead, is purely coincidental and not intended by the author.
All brand names and product names used in this book are trademarks, registered trademarks, or trade names of their respective holders. Green Dragon Publishing is not associated with any product or vendor in this book.

Published by Green Dragon Publishing
Beacon Falls, CT
www.GreenDragonArtist.com
All rights reserved.

TABLE OF CONTENTS

Introduction
Contributors

PART ONE: The Planning Stage
Chapter One: Planning versus Pantsing
Chapter Two: In the Beginning: The Concept
Chapter Three: Research All the Things
Chapter Four: Synopsis
Chapter Five: Character Deep Dive
Chapter Six: Setting the Scene… List

PART TWO: The First Draft
Chapter Seven: Opening Scene
Chapter Eight: The Frightening Blank Page
Chapter Nine: Dialogue vs. Narrative vs. Action
Chapter Ten: Scene by Scene
Chapter Eleven: Characters Gone Awry
Chapter Twelve: The Agony and the Ecstasy
Chapter Thirteen: The Dreaded Writers' Block
Chapter Fourteen: Procrastination and the Finished First Draft

PART THREE: Evil Editing
Chapter Fifteen: Editing Types
Chapter Sixteen: First Round of Edits and All the Pain
Chapter Seventeen: Draft Number Two, Electric Bugaloo
Chapter Eighteen: Beta Readers or How to Alienate Your Friends and Family

PART FOUR: TRADITIONAL PUBLISHING PATH
Chapter Nineteen: The Querying Process

Chapter Twenty: Submissions
Chapter Twenty-One: Acceptance and More Editing
Chapter Twenty-Two: Artist Package, ARCs, and Review Requests, Oh, My!

PART FIVE: SELF-PUBLISHING PATH
Chapter Twenty-Three: Formatting Hell
Chapter Twenty-Four: Judging a Book by its Cover
Chapter Twenty-Five: To Audio or Not To Audio?
Chapter Twenty-Six: So Many Publishing Platforms

PART SIX: THE HEADY AFTERMATH
Chapter Twenty-Seven: Release the Kraken!
Chapter Twenty-Eight: Begging for Reviews (More Ways to Alienate your Friends and Family)
Chapter Twenty-Nine: Selling Yourself

Conclusion
Resources
Thank You and Links
Other Books by Christy Nicholas
Author's Note
About the Author

INTRODUCTION

Staring at a blank page. Every author's nightmare.

It doesn't need to be more frightening than a Stephen King book. No, really! I'm serious. Stop laughing.

While most authors of novels are intimidated by the enormous task before them, that intimidation can be chopped up into quivering bits with some planning and task management.

I must confess a secret. I didn't plan my first book. I didn't plan my second book. Not even my third. Now, now, stop clutching at your pearls. The truth is, I cheated on all three of those.

My first two books weren't novels. They were travel guides. The reason I cheated was because I had already written much of the books before I ever considered publishing them. I'd been to Ireland and Scotland several times each and had taken copious real-time notes in the form of trip reports. This was both for my own flawed memory and to share the trip with others on a vicarious basis.

Several people had asked for advice on trip planning themselves, so I'd written up several cheat sheets for how to find a good B&B, or car rental, or researching airfare. I therefore compiled this data, as well as my notes from sites I'd visited, and added some I researched. Voila! A travel guide.

Which brings me to my first novel. I didn't know anything about planning a novel. I didn't know anything about writing a novel. I just knew I needed to write that novel, the story of my parents' thirty-year search for true love, which culminated in a wedding on the Starship Enterprise in Las Vegas.

So, I dove right in. I wrote a few scenes in order, hated them, tried again. Then I tossed those and tried it from another angle. And again. Then I got tired of that crap and just kept writing.

However, this was all a cheat. No, really, it was. This was a novel based on a true story, so I knew the salient details, I knew the characters, I knew how it ended… none of that was anything I had to create. It was handed to me on a silver platter, not a real test of my plotting ability.

After the first draft, I decided I wanted to add a second point of view, that of my own as the researcher who found her father after thirty years, when he didn't even know he had a child. So, I went back to add all that in.

In the end, I had a relatively cohesive tale, but the editing was atrocious. However, I didn't realize it, and published it with a friend's micro-publishing company. Many years later, I've gotten the rights to the novel back, and rewrote it, knowing what I've learned about writing in the meantime, and republished. I was in a state of permanent face-palm reading the first version. Not planning, and not properly editing, had led to so many continuity errors, outright contradictions, and plot holes, I'm amazed anyone liked it.

Now, not everyone is a planner. Some people prefer "pantsing," or writing by the seat of their pants. Another term I like for this technique is "discovery writing." If you prefer that way, you may be thinking, "Planning: blah, blah, blah, outline, blah, blah, blah."

Most authors are on a spectrum somewhere between Extreme Pantser and Extreme Planner. But I think most authors could find some useful tools in this book, tools which might allow them to sculpt that horrifying prospect into digestible chunks.

Sorry for the graphic imagery. I guess Stephen King is still on my mind.

Please keep in mind that this book just demonstrates some ways in which authors can plan, write, and publish their books. It's novel-centric, planner-centric, historical fiction-centric, and me-centric. I am in no way putting forth that this is the only way to write, or even to plan, a novel. As the saying goes, your mileage may vary.

The process of writing a novel is a scary mystery to most people. Sometimes including those who actually write novels! My own process is just one of thousands of processes, but here is a peek into my mad method.

CONTRIBUTORS

No one writes in a vacuum. Editors, beta readers, author friends, and resources all simmer in an author's mind to distill into the final product. I've gotten some fantastic input from my beta readers, such as Ian Erik Morris and author Lee O'Connell, as well as authors Mattea Orr and Joseph Crance on some of this material, and their help has been invaluable.

In addition, I've done lots of research online, gathering data from places like Writer's Digest, Reedsy, Ads for Authors, Writer's Beware, and Absolute Write Water Cooler. Nothing proprietary, of course, but general information that might be helpful for the budding author.

The author group I am part of has been the most help, allowing me to see how my process was different from others. This group was organized and is run by fellow author Melora Johnson and has been the single most invaluable tool I've had as an author.

PART ONE: THE PLANNING STAGE

CHAPTER ONE: PLANNING VERSUS PANTSING

> **PLANNER:** One who creates a writing plan before and/or during their writing process
>
> **PANTSER:** One who writes "by the seat of their pants," allowing creativity to guide their story during the writing process

I am a planner. That doesn't mean I am rigidly required to adhere to my plan, but I do make a plan and mostly follow it. No one is 100% pantser or planner, rather most writers are on the spectrum between those extremes. Despite my adoration for a well-crafted plan, that plan has run afoul of my story many times. One scene becomes eight, eight becomes one. Subplots take a left turn. New characters show up out of the blue and just demand to be added, sometimes taking entire subplots as their own.

It's madness.

However, that doesn't mean I won't plan the next book. I just hold in my heart the understanding that the best laid plans of writers and authors must be modified as required. Just like any war, tactics change as the battlefield conditions do.

So, whether you see yourself "Full of Pants" or a "Plan-loving Word Bug," settle in and enjoy.

CHAPTER TWO:
IN THE BEGINNING: CONCEPT

Inciting incident – a change in a character's normal life that thrusts them into the main action of the story

I strongly believe in teaching by example. Therefore, I'll be using a book I wrote, Misfortune of Vision as a step-by-step guide. Misfortune of Vision is the fourth novel in the Druid's Brooch series. Book two, Legacy of Truth, had just been published the month I started Misfortune of Vision, and book three, Legacy of Luck, was submitted and due out four months later.

The idea was to have three trilogies in total for a total of nine books in the series, because I am wedded to symmetry. The first trilogy (the Legacy books) is set in the 18th/19th century. The second trilogy (the Misfortune books) are set in the 11th/12th century. The third and final trilogy (the Age books) are set in the 5th/6th century, and the final book of that trilogy gives the origins of the brooch itself.

That means to plan my next book, I really must plan out six novels. And make them all tie neatly into a bow at the end. Right. Okay, deep breath, let it out easily. Let's do this.

Most writers are Planners or Plotters to some extent. I'm strong on the Planner end of the spectrum. That means I like to plan out my book and my scenes, flesh out my characters and my subplots before the first word is written. Yes, it can change later due to the capriciousness of my muse and my own editing, but that's how I begin. When I got into planning, I used The Snowflake Method (an amazing process you can look up online, though I have no affiliation with the creator). This process was a delight to this detail-oriented accountant/author. I've modified my process since then to suit my own style, which I encourage everyone to do. Find a method that works for yourself.

My first task is to come up with a basic premise for each book. A one-sentence elevator pitch, or what you'd say to an agent if you ended up on an elevator with them and only had a few minutes to pitch your book.

Using some popular novels for examples:
- **Outlander**: 1940s nurse travels back in time 200 years and falls in love with a Highlander in the Jacobite revolution.
- **Lord of the Rings**: A group of farmers embark on a quest with a wizard and some elves to destroy an object of evil in a fantasy realm.
- **Hunger Games**: A girl volunteers to fight to be the last person standing in a brutal entertainment show to save her sister.
-

As you work on your own one-sentence elevator pitch, concentrate on the meat of the concept, not the details. Ignore names for now. No subplots. No side characters. Make those few minutes count without wasting it with extraneous add-ons.

- Describe what your protagonist does. (the Character)
- What changes in their world to start off the story? (the Inciting Incident)
- What do they need to accomplish? (the Goal)
- What do they lose if they fail? (the Stakes)

Each basic pitch should have a main character, an overarching conflict, a goal, and stakes.

The Character: Form a brief description. Gender? Age? Physical description? Motivation? Personality quirk? Nothing deep yet, just something quick and dirty for now.

For Misfortune of Vision, my main character is a 65-year-old grandmother. One inspiration for my character was a reddit thread about the savior of the world needing to be a grandmother with life skills rather than yet another teenage wonder child. Sure, I won't be able to include as much angst and rebellion, but I can insert plenty of snark and sarcasm. I love it when little old ladies order everyone else around.

CHARACTER EXERCISE: Describe your main character. How old are they? How heavy? What color is their skin? Their eyes? What is their hair like? Do they pick their lips? Bite their fingernails? How do they present their gender?

The Inciting Incident: What changes in their normal life to make them interesting enough to write a story? Does someone come to town? Do they go on a quest? Does their father figure die in a horrible fire? Do *they* die? (i.e., The Lovely Bones) Something gets them out of "ordinary" and into conflict.

The inciting incident will be her giving a dire prophecy that no one believes. A classic Cassandra tale. And, of course, it's about an incident that means personal, physical danger, not only to her, but everyone she knows.

INCITING INCIDENT EXERCISE: Where does your main character live? What's a typical day like? What is their job? Who do they live with? What happens to change that everyday life? What event from their past haunts them?

The Goal: What is their purpose in this conflict? To survive? To win a race? To marry the hunk next door? To save their best friend from an alien?

My little old lady needs a quest, so she's seeking out an heir. Why? Well, she has this heirloom. A magic brooch she must gift to a relative, which is a common element through "The Druid's Brooch Series" To raise the stakes, all her children are dead, so she must seek out her grandchildren. She either has never met them or hasn't seen them since they were babies, because travel in the twelfth century was dangerous and tedious.

GOAL EXERCISE: What does your main character want more than anything in the world? What goal drives them to shove off the daily drone and do something about it? What catalyzes them into action? Why now?

The Stakes: What happens if they don't reach that goal? Will they be left in a loveless marriage? Will the world go *poof* into a million atoms? Will their hair fall out?

If she doesn't pass on the brooch, it will be lost to the human world forever. Her family passed this legacy to her, and she must uphold her honor.

STAKES EXERCISE: What will your main character lose if they don't reach their goal? At what point in the story does this become the point of no return?

If you're writing a series, like I am, it might be a good idea to work out your main elevator-pitch plot on the other books-to-be, so you have a good variety of themes and plots. I did a one-paragraph synopsis on each of the eight remaining books after I finished book one, so I didn't run out of ideas and have to change something I'd already done. See? Extreme planning!

Once you've got a one-sentence elevator pitch, you can use that in the future to tempt an agent or write advertising copy. For now, you'll use it as the seed to grow your synopsis.

ELEVATOR PITCH EXERCISE: Combine the above exercises into an elevator pitch, one sentence that describes your character, the setting, their goal, and the stakes. It can be a long sentence, but must be able to be said in ten seconds.

CHAPTER THREE:
RESEARCH ALL THE THINGS

This section is going to be very historical fiction oriented. However, most novels set in the real world, including contemporaries, romances, and literary, require some research to properly ground your readers in setting. Even if you're setting your book in your own hometown, like a memoir, you will need to research some details to improve verisimilitude.

If you're creating a science fiction or fantasy realm, then you need to do even more research. You'll want to create magic systems that work, or a socioeconomic world in space exploration. Do you need to know more about black holes? Faster-than-light drives? How about the power structure of a medieval setting with seven types of sentient creatures vying for primacy? Do they each have their own cultures, languages, and martial traditions? Don't forget maps! For examples of extreme planners, see Frank Herbert, Patrick Rothfuss, or J.R.R. Tolkien.

So, that's a huge amount of planning. Where does one start? That really depends on your personal passion. If you love politics, you might start crafting the political structure of your world. If you love travel or geography, you might begin with a physical setting. If you love history, you might first find a real historical event to base your story around.

I love history. I needed to find a time of great conflict to set my story in.

For Misfortune of Vision, since it's set in the twelfth century, I dove into a rabbit hole of the Annals of Irish History, Lady Gregory, Yeats, and the ever-mocked Wikipedia. Yes, you can use Wikipedia, but please be cautious of using that as a source.

While Wikipedia can be a great tool to give a researcher a path to more reliable sources, I prefer to use those resources when I can access them. I don't rely on Wikipedia's accuracy. People can change the information at any time, without any sources. At the bottom of the page, there are often links or lists to the source data. Many are scholarly resources, peer-reviewed or published. Often, I can find a great article listed there but hosted on sites such as academia.edu or jstor.com to help me get the historical details I need. Unfortunately, I must add a caveat that some of these reliable resources are behind a pay wall. However, sometimes if you can find the article you need, you can contact the author and they will send you a copy.

As an example, I researched kings and social structure. I spent way too much time finding a better word for king, since that was not a word used for Celtic people in the twelfth century. I looked up documents about the time period, including the Annals of Ireland. I asked some scholars I know on the period about their suggestions. After sifting through many bad options from other cultures, I finally found one which fit with Irish culture of the time: Chief or Chieftain.

Then I researched clergy and local saints, which melded into fairy queens and holy wells. I found maps of sacred sites in Ireland, as well as the history of the larger ones. I delved into Neolithic mounds and burnt villages in the area, since I wanted my character to encounter the Fae in a mystical spot. Neolithic mounds and stone circles were the best places for such encounters. Burnt villages were a great backdrop for tragedy and violence.

After a good fifteen hours' worth of research (no, I'm not exaggerating), I checked out the local Vikings, to see if it was logical to include them as an added conflicting element and what they were called. In the records of the time, people called them Ostmen or simply Foreigners. I discovered a local chief who was a renowned craven coward. When the Norman invasion reached the northern counties, he simply fled.

Fantastic! Cowardly chiefs are great! Let's use him. He was the Chief in Downpatrick, but John de Courci, a famous Norman, took the town. Now I know where my main character lives, and exactly when the story would take place. She has a purpose and plenty of crap to get in the way of that purpose.

External conflict is easier to meld into the characters' internal conflict, adding tension and action. When I decided on twelfth century Ireland, I had no idea exactly how violent this time was in the northeast of Ireland. I knew atrocities happened in the southeast with the Norman invasion, but this time period makes Game of

Thrones look like a peaceful Sunday picnic. Perfect for high tension stories.

SOURCES

The main historically reliable documents from the time, such as the Annals of Ulster, mostly just list the deaths of chiefs and nobles, bishops, and other Very Important Personages. There were a lot of them! It seemed like every minor chief had a relative who hated him enough to off him for his throne. Some were details about cattle raids, sieges, or a kidnapping, but the majority were the stark mortality details.

However, once you get your hands on a juicy, historically accurate conflict, some historical characters you can work into your story, and a concrete time period, you can plop your characters into the middle and see if they swim.

> Your tale is more interesting if your characters can't swim.

I went back to do some editing on a previous manuscript to give my unconscious mind time to percolate the story. As I did so, I realized that I've already read several books set in my time period by authors whose research I respect. Ken Follett (Pillars of the Earth), Sir Walter Scott (Ivanhoe), and Ellis Peters (Brother Cadfael Mysteries) have written books set in the twelfth century.

While they were all set in England, a different culture and political structure, they still give me some "flavor" of the setting, mores of the day, and details about daily life at that level of technology and trade.

For some people, anything prior to modern times is "ancient" and there is little differentiation between those periods. For an historian, however, or an enthusiast of historical fiction, those differences are important. And I won't even get into the debate over the misnomer "Dark Ages" here because I don't want this book to be 100,000 words long.

For instance, a noblewoman of seventeenth century France would wear a completely different costume than a noblewoman in twelfth century France. The Renaissance occurred at different times in different areas throughout Europe, and took different forms throughout the world, just as the Bronze and Iron Ages did. Technology and fashion took time to migrate in the past, as social media hadn't quite been invented yet.

When writing details of the time period, an author could research the different foods a character is eating (Pro tip: Your 12th century character wouldn't order a caramel frappe from Starbucks!), clothing, the way they made their living, etc. Even within professions, they might have different names, such as a wheelwright or cooper. At the same time, you need to ensure your modern reader understands the reference. Make certain that unfamiliar terms are couched in context, or have a glossary in the book.

> Planning allows the author to create a complex web of subplots to weave around your main conflict, each one adding to the overall tension of the tale.

These differences in culture can help a lot in your planning. Different time periods, cultures, even different worlds, can offer a variety of interesting conflict to assist in your plot and make your characters miserable.

I then make a list of possible conflicts that arise from such an environment. There are both internal and external conflicts.

Internal conflicts might be a moral dilemma, a crisis of faith, or the suspicion of a friend or family member. Someone might be dealing with PTSD, depression, or anger management.

External conflicts might include that broken wagon wheel, war, or someone blocking the road. A broken wagon wheel wasn't as easily fixed as a flat tire is today. An arranged marriage was much more common for nobility in medieval times. Blasphemy was a huge worry.

CONFLICT EXERCISE: List out at least three possible internal and external conflicts in your story.
    External
    - Physical Conflicts (actions)
    Internal
    - Emotional Conflicts (feelings)
    - Philosophical Conflicts (beliefs, values)

DIALOGUE

Speech and idiom are the hardest parts to get right. It's a balancing act. Of course, the twelfth century Irish character isn't speaking anything resembling English. They aren't even speaking modern Irish. They're speaking middle or archaic Irish, and no one today outside of a few scholars would easily be able to read it. I certainly wouldn't be able to write it. Even if it was set in England, twelfth century language is very different from today's English. If you doubt me, go read some Anglo-Norman works. Beowulf dates a few centuries earlier and is almost incomprehensible to the untrained modern reader. Most folks today can puzzle out Chaucer's writing, which was several hundred years later. English as a language was a proto-mix of Germanic from Anglo-Saxon peasants and French from Norman nobles with a sprinkling of ecclesiastical Latin thrown in for seasoning.

So, I use mostly modern English in historical novels. But I don't use pure modern English, as that would sound strange with idiom, changing word meanings, etc. Telling someone that the assassin was going to "pop a cap" in their victim's head just seems… wrong to me.

Now, some stories get by with modern usage. Shows like Spartacus or Reign have done it to good effect. However, it must be done well or it comes across as flat. Also, idiom and slang common to historical periods can be used, as long as you ensure your reader knows what they mean in modern terms.

As Good Omens by Gaiman and Pratchett point out, the word "nice" used to mean foolish, then particular, and now, something pleasant. Words, even within one language, change meaning over time.

Even if you aren't writing historical novels, each character should have their own voice. The reader should be able to pick out a character by what they say, even if you don't tell them who is talking.

Most historical fiction authors sprinkle older words and phrases into modern English and try to limit the anachronisms to give a flavor of the time. Sometimes this is easy – often it isn't. It involves a lot of research, delving into resources such as Etymonline.com (an online dictionary of word and term origins, including sources and dates first found) and historical theses.

Once you've written in a particular time period, you get a feel for the language. You can add a couple of words or phrases to your characters' lexicon.

> Gift your main characters with pet phrases, exclamations, and curses that reflect the flavor of the time.

If you've done this well, your reader is transported to their time and place.

There is always a danger of putting in too much flavor. Have you ever had a dish that was so heavily spiced that all you tasted was the seasoning, and not the food itself? Some writing ends up like that, where you have to sound out the words on the page to make any sense of what was being said. I've seen some too-accurate Glasgow accents written this way. Or Cockney. Or in the American deep south. Just remember – less is more! And please don't use phrases like "Avast ye, knavish varlet!"

Incidentally, this concept also works with accents. A light dose of phrases or pronunciation changes goes a long way. Too much, and the dialogue is difficult to read.

There is a historical fiction author whose books are well-loved by thousands of readers. They were set in a time period I liked, and I tried my best to enjoy them. However, the author's use of vernacular and random phrases in obscure foreign languages, such as Old French or Lowland Scots, was so prevalent, I had a difficult time reading her stories. This was in the 1990s, before the advent of easy translation software, so when a phrase popped up without context, I had no way of knowing what it meant. Enough of that, and I gave up.

SWEARING

Swearing is an area that is particularly difficult. A modern person swears differently than someone in the eighteenth century, sixteenth century, or the fifth century would. In the past, most swearing was religious in nature – "Zounds," used liberally by Shakespeare, was short for "God's Wounds." Now, in a society less dominated by religion, we use words more related to physical body functions.

Some cultures, such as the Scottish and Irish I tend to write in, have a lovely tradition of cursing in creative ways. One such Irish curse is "May the devil make a ladder of your backbone and pluck apples in the garden of hell." This is delightfully evocative.

> **PET PHRASE EXERCISE:** What does your character say when they stub their toe? What do they say when they are angry at someone? What do they say when they're thrilled?

ANACHRONISMS

These are little things that must be kept in mind as you're writing your manuscript. Little but important. A glaring anachronism can push a reader right out of the story, and their suspense of disbelief shattered.

Often small discrepancies can be forgiven (like rose madder being used to dye cloth in the twelfth century when it didn't become popular until the thirteenth in Pillars of the Earth). These are details only a historian or pedant will care about. Others, not so much (like horned helmets on Vikings), as it's getting more well known that they never wore those. Don't make your twelfth century character a Baptist, as Protestantism started in the 16th century.

LOCATION, LOCATION, LOCATION

Where do you place your story?

They say to "write what you know." If that were entirely true, there would be no such thing as speculative fiction, science fiction, or fantasy. However, to some extent it does hold true. Writing about a place you are intimately familiar with can help with details.

Incidentally, if you are writing in speculative fiction, science fiction, or fantasy, your planning opportunities increase incredibly. You can plan entire worlds, cultures, histories, languages. Just ask Tolkien! He created a language and then decided to write novels using it as a cultural detail.

I mostly write about Ireland. Do I live there? No. But my ancestors did. Well, some of them. 11% of them, according to my DNA test. However, I have visited many times, and Ireland holds a piece of my soul. I love putting details in my writing from the places I've been, and it helps to add realism to the story.

For example, I've stayed in a town called Ardara in County Donegal. I was able to picture exactly how the town was set up, with the main streets forming a Y through the center. I used this setting for both Legacy of Hunger and Legacy of Truth.

Since most of my books are set in historical time periods, I do research to see what was actually there at the time. The grand cathedral in the center of the market town may have been built in 1848, and my book is set in 1846, so maybe I have a construction site, but no finished building. The hotel was in business, and the pub, so I used them in my story. I researched the local standing stones to find one or two to feature as part of the tale, too. These details are important to me. They might not matter to most of my readers, but I do get anxiety thinking about the few who might care.

How do you find such details? Sometimes it's difficult to research the history of places. Buildings such as churches can be easier, as most churches are proud of their building's age. You may have to dig a little, but usually the Catholic church keeps good track of such things. If you write early enough, no buildings are on record. For instance, I'm working on a novel called The Enchanted Swans, which starts in 500 BCE. No Christian churches existed in Ireland then. Of course, there were lots of buildings – roundhouses and crannogs. But few were made of stone, mostly wooden palisades. A physical or virtual visit to Craggaunowen or Navan Fort can help with the visualization of such structures.

Landscape doesn't change much over time. Sure, bits of cliff may fall into the ocean, or mountain tops are leveled for a tourist view, but for the most part, Conor's Pass in Dingle offers a similar view to what it's had for a thousand years. And having been to that view – three times before I could see anything due to heavy mists – I can describe the sublime landscape view in a novel.

In my novels Legacy of Hunger and Legacy of Truth, the story is set partially in Donegal, Achill Island, and Kenmare. I've been to each of these places, and therefore have a better handle on the geography, distance between places, and the challenges of living in such an environment.

No matter where your imagination takes you, make sure to know the place before you try to transport others there. Even if it's only research via old photographs, paintings, or Google Earth, there is a way to make sure the details come through and become part of your story.

When I determine the location for my story, I start with Googlemaps Streetview, and look around the place. I look at both modern and historical photos, if I can find them. If I'm writing about a particular building, I try to find when it was built.

SETTING EXERCISE: What does your setting have that's unique? Is it a seaside town? A mountain chalet? A spaceship heading into the sun?

CHAPTER FOUR: SYNOPSIS

Once you've written a one-sentence summary of your novel, and conducted some research into your world-building, then you can expand that to a full paragraph.

The sentences should have the basic plot, the setting, the time period, the character.

> **EXERCISE:** Expand your one sentence into three sentences. One to set up the 'daily life' and character, one to introduce the conflict, and one to identify the stakes. Once you've got those three, you can mix them up so they flow better.

I'd seen a meme about a reader being tired of books where the Chosen One was always an angsty teenager who saved the world. I decided my main character would be a grandmother with attitude. She must be someone with power, with strength. Therefore, I made her a Seer, someone with a magical power. This fit in perfectly with my series, where each main character who held the Druid's Brooch was granted some magical power.

I needed to take my Seer and give her some conflicts. The first is, of course, the prophecy itself. When she foresees disaster for her home, she isn't believed. It's a trope, but a common one thanks to our addiction to Greek myths. The most logical person not to believe her is the Chief.

My character is a rare thing – a woman of some power in medieval Europe. She's not used to being dismissed, or her counsel being ignored. Her reaction to being disbelieved is to leave. However, she's still concerned about the people in her home, a place she's lived all her life. So, she does leave – but she goes on a quest to find a solution.

But wait, I needed a disaster for her to foresee! A war? An invasion? Let's go with invasion for now. There might be Vikings nearby in the twelfth century, right? I'll do some research after I get the bones set up.

Let's add an external conflict. It's the dead of winter in the north of Ireland. No one of advanced age is going to have an easy time traveling in the ice and snow.

A Seer near retirement in twelfth century Ireland foresees an invasion. She must embark on a quest to find her heir before the invaders arrive, but no one believes her prophecy. Without the support of her chief, she goes off on her own in the dead of winter.

> That one paragraph should now grow to three paragraphs with main characters and plot line,
> a few side characters and maybe even a hint at subplots.

Your basic outline should include a minimum of these:
- Story setup (a character's typical life before stuff hits the fan)
- Several strong obstacles
  - You can use a 3-act structure, each worse than the last, bonus points if the character's own poor decisions make each one worse
- Ending of novel (resolution of the character's quest)

You can create this from the climax and work your way into the smaller details:
- What big event catalyzes the character into action now?
- What is the midpoint of the story, the point of no return, or a point where the character has an epiphany?
- What is the lowest point, the place where your character has to dig into their soul to risk everything?
- What is the climax, the final face-off where the character fights their opposition?

Alternatively, you can create this from the smaller details and work your way up:

- What is your main character's normal life before the catalyst? (Example: Life in the Shire is sweet)
- What incident (catalyst) shakes them out of their normal life? (Example: Gandalf arrives to take Frodo on a quest)
- What is your main character's main goal?
  - What are their mini-goals, the things they must achieve to get to this goal? (Example: They must get to the Prancing Pony, they must escape the Ring-Wraiths, they must make it to Rivendell)
  - What is in the way of each of these mini-goals? (Example: The ring calls to the Ring-Wraiths. Gandalf doesn't meet them)
- From the mini-goals, what are some major highs or lows? Which can be intensified for higher drama/conflict? (Example: When Frodo wakes in Rivendell, he sees all his friends and Bilbo as well)
- What is your character's 'all is lost' moment, the time when everything seems the darkest? (Example: The battle of Helm's Deep, just before Gandalf arrives)
- Climax – The big battle, the ultimate pay-off the entire novel has been working up to. This should have the highest stakes, the most to lose, and shouldn't be an easy win.
- Resolution – tying up the loose story ends.

THEME

A theme is an overarching message (no need to be preachy) of what your character believes in, such as loyalty (blood is thicker than water), faith (the universe will come through in the end), honor (the whole is more important than the individual), or love (romance is worth the heartbreak). This theme should be challenged by the protagonist, and it may change over time for both the protagonist and the antagonist.

How do you pick a theme? What do you care about? What value do you want your story to spotlight? What about your protagonist? Is there a particular theme that your existing audience loves?

Braveheart is an obvious example. It highlighted the concept of freedom. The Scarlet Letter has a theme of justice, as does To Kill a Mockingbird. Lord of the Flies uses survival. Lord of the Rings uses both heroism and good and evil. Many of Shakespeare's plays center around betrayal.

A good conclusion that is true to your theme helps the reader feel like the story has been worth it. It also helps you, as the author, figure out what to include in your climax and what sort of decisions your characters need to make at that point. The climax represents the big decision for your character, a make it or break it moment. This may result in a change in beliefs or values.

SUBPLOTS AND SECONDARY CHARACTERS

Now, it's time to add in some subplots and secondary characters. Mine is a historical fantasy series, and there are Fae involved, so let's bring one into the plotline. Also, let's give her some responsibility. An orphan! Everyone loves orphans. How is her quest going to save the world? I don't know yet. So, let's shift to a subplot.

Orlagh has this magical brooch, and she knows she needs to pass it onto a family member. That's the rule. Therefore, she goes to find her heir. I can't make that easy, so her children are all dead, and she's barely met her grandchildren, as they moved away. Did I mention Vikings before? My research shows they did live nearby but weren't very much into raiding at that point. More of a settlement than an invading force. However, a Norman army did invade. I can use that!

A Seer near retirement in twelfth century Ireland delivers a prophecy of invasion to her Chief. However, he doesn't believe her, and she leaves in a huff of temper. A Fae associate tells her she must find an heir, as her time is coming near.

In the dead of winter, she takes her ward and embarks on a quest to find her grandchildren, as her children have died. On the way, she runs afoul Vikings, an enemy Norman camp, and an insane Fae Lord.

When she finally defeats those who oppose her, and just as her dire prophecy comes true, she finds her heir and delivers her destiny.

EXERCISE: Expand your three sentences into three paragraphs.

- The first paragraph should introduce the character, setting, and basic conflict. It can add a supporting character or two and mention the stakes.
- The second paragraph should include complications in the original conflict, actions which make things worse, and the character's intended solution to this problem.
- The third paragraph will describe the resolution of the character's quest.

Now that I've got a three-paragraph synopsis (barely), I expand each paragraph into fuller paragraphs. I add more subplots, more characters to help the main character on her quest. Does she have a love interest? Not really. Not every book needs one. And I want to make her kick-ass and sarcastic, not doe-eyed and falling in love. But I might add an old campaigner who's an old friend and good in a fight. I've got one Fae as a friend and another as foe. I can have fun entwining their stories and motivations into hers. I add other characters and barriers to make her life even more difficult.

Each of the main characters get at least a few paragraphs of physical description, personality traits, pet phrases, and family relations. Even the secondary characters get a few details. This way, when they show up again, I don't have to remember if I made them blond or brunette.

In the end, this is what I end up with for my synopsis, roughly 1500 words.

Orlagh must give the chief a prophecy, but all she sees is war, death and destruction in the coming years. The bishop (Malachi III) is fearful of her, and resents her power with the chief, urging him to banish her. She uses theatrics for her prophecies, but she doesn't need to, as it's a native magic through a magic brooch. She doesn't wish to be punished for her gloomy forecasts, so she couches them in ambiguous terms. Luckily, the chief doesn't call on her often, as he is more concerned with building additions to the new nearby Augustinian monastery (Erenagh), urged by his bishop. She has developed a prejudice against the Bishop but can do nothing about his influence.

Declan was working for a local farmer, but two years of disastrous crops forced the farmer to let him go. He practically starves trying to beg and steals to survive. He heard about some soldiers passing through, but they were actually Ostmen, having settled in Strangford Lough (Strangfyorthe). Declan took cleaning work as he had no other options but tried in little ways to sabotage his employers. He was skilled at singing, but the Ostmen didn't appreciate his songs. He meets another servant, Hellevi, and they develop a relationship. One of the Ostmen (blacksmith) like Hellevi and wants her to be his. She refuses, and he's abusive. Declan vows to protect her. She loves his singing.

Orlagh has no close friends, but cares for a young orphan girl, Clodagh, to whom she is attempting to teach the art of prophecy. Orlagh's three sons were killed years ago, but she starts having dreams about her grandson. She is on an errand for the chief and has an encounter with Adhna, a blind wise man living inside a yew tree, who reminds her she must bequeath her magical druid's brooch to someone of her bloodline. Declan went off years ago to follow the soldiers, making his living from their cast-offs.

One of Declan's sabotage efforts is discovered by his rival. He was mixing in some ash to the blacksmith's mix, in order that the swords break more easily. The blacksmith attacks him, and he defends himself. He is almost killed, but he injures the blacksmith. He has no money for weregeld, and no family to pay it for him. He is almost sentenced to death, but is skilled tongue argues him out of it and into banishment instead. He and Hellevi wander again until he finds another.

Amidst rumors that the Normans have left traveling north from Dublin, Orlagh travels south into the center of the turmoil to find

Declan. She loses Clodagh at one point but finds her Adhna. The old man gives the seer some advice she doesn't want to take but tells her that she can lose the legacy if she doesn't find a proper heir. This scares Orlagh, and she chases many rumors and uses her own talent to seek Declan out.

She finally finds Declan just as he's been arrested in the Norman's camp being framed for stealing but manages to use her authority as the chief's Seer to save him from the noose. She has a battle of wills with the Bishop. She introduces him to some of the pagan elements in Celtic Christianity. She is bombarded with visions of disaster to the point they almost cripple her, and she tries to warn the bishop. He is too optimistic that he can avert disaster and dismisses her warnings.

Orlagh finds her grandson and talks to him about the brooch. Declan is so angry about someone trying to frame him that Orlagh second-guesses her duty with the brooch. Then he decides he wants the brooch after all and tries to take it from her when she declines to gift it to him. She leaves in disgust, and he leaves Hellevi to track after his grandmother. Orlagh seeks out a stone circle to ask for guidance from the Fae in desperation. A Fae noble, Ammatán, answers her call, and says he has an answer, but she must complete a task for her.

Ammatán's quest says she must find the lost rath of Emain Macha and extract an artifact from under the mound. The artifact is a musical instrument, a harp given to a shallow man Orlagh once loved, long ago in her youth. It had been a gift by Ammatán, a gift given on the basis of his friendship with her family. The harp had previously been gifted to Amergin by Banba, the local Fae queen.

The news of the rousting of Dunleavy at Down reaches them. Orlagh is torn between going to help her people and continuing on her quest, but the cowardice of her chief decides the issue. He has run, and she can do nothing about that.

Hellevi urges Declan to go after his grandmother to recover the brooch which is his by right. He argues himself out of the fear and decides he's angry at his grandmother's rejection of him, Declan takes Hellevi and goes to Emain Macha. Seeing they are within the mound he loosens rocks to keep them there and then sends Hellevi to fetch nearby Norse warriors. Declan hopes to ask for the brooch as a reward for his deliverance of Clodagh as a slave, as well as get back into the good graces of the Ostmen.

Orlagh, Cu-Uladh, and Clodagh escape the mound, but are waylaid by Ostmen. The Ostmen first threaten to take the child, but Orlagh threatens to tell them the date of their death to frighten them. Declan argues against her skill, calling her a sham, but they don't quite believe him. They apologize and offer to buy Clodagh, but Orlagh refuses. Then she pushes her prophecy into telepathy, but that is painful to her, but impressive to the Ostmen, who still believe in the Old Gods despite their conversion to Christianity. They think her a personification of a Norn, and leave while they can, taking Declan and Hellevi with them as slaves instead. They believe offering him up as a sacrifice will appease the Gods he's angered. Hellevi cries as she's married off to the blacksmith. They burn Declan, and he dies screaming Hellevi's name.

In the end, Ammatán tells her that Clodagh is actually her own great-granddaughter, a by-blow from her younger sister. Orlagh decides to gift the brooch to Clodagh.

Ammatán wishes to take Orlagh back to the Otherworld, but she refuses. He threatens to take Clodagh instead, so she sacrifices herself for her great-granddaughter. But first, they agree she can go back to Ballynoe to prime Clodagh with the brooch. On the way, they try to find a way to break the agreement. She helps heal Clodagh and her abuse issues but cannot succeed in breaking the agreement despite the use of magic. Cu-Uladh tries to argue her out of it, but then makes her promise to wait for him in Faerie. She travels to the otherworld and sees her new home in the Fae land.

PLOT AND SUBPLOTS

How do you add plots and subplots, you ask? I am so glad you asked! There are lots of ways to get ideas, but here are some basics. You can get inspiration from other stories, real life, or your imagination running wild. Mix those other story elements with new ones and you've got a brand-new plot.

PLOT
- Someone goes on a journey (Boy off in search of adventure)
- A stranger arrives (Gunman in an old west town)
- Something goes wrong (Asteroid coming for earth)
- Headline (real or parody)
- Search for a MacGuffin (intrinsic object: Holy Grail, One Ring)

CHARACTER
- Coming of age (most Young Adult novels)

- Marriage/Death/Birth
- Fish out of water (My Fair Lady)

WHAT IF?
- Change of historical fact/person (Jesus never lived, or Hitler won)
- New technology/magic (The Saint: Cold Fusion)
- Disaster response (Independence Day)

MORE CONSIDERATIONS
- You shouldn't start your scene list (more about that next!) until you know your Hero, World, and Hook (also explained later). Where the book begins, what the inciting incident is, what the main conflict is, what the climax is, and how it ends. If you can aim for at least planning these major points you're much more likely to hit all the places/beats/emotions/scenes you want to because you know where you're going.
- Start at the inciting incident. Figure out what happens that changes this person's life and sets them on the path that will lead to your climax and ending. From there, you can work backwards to the beginning.
    - Side note: It is perfectly fine to write the first scene and completely change it when you're done with your book! In fact, that's how it normally works for me. You are much more familiar with the story and the characters at that point, and your opening scene is so important, it must be impactful.

- The beginning should usually be a short time before the inciting incident, should show us your main character at a level of action that brings the reader into the story, and reveals something of their strength/s and weakness/es.
- When figuring out the climax, think about how to construct it around your main character's strengths and weaknesses. This is the most pivotal moment in the book. Milk it for all it's worth because the journey from inciting incident to climax is your character arc. Use the same ideas when considering your "villain." You want to give them agency and depth, as well as stronger power than the protagonist. Agency is when the main character's decisions (good or bad) drive the action of the narrative. When your character doesn't have agency, things just happen to them and they react. When they do have agency, they are in control of their story. If their decisions in one climax create the climate for the second one, especially if it was a bad decision, that leads to a more exciting narrative.
- Flawed main character + inciting incident = motivation to change. Main character struggles against what is standing in their way until they reach the climax, which should be constructed for them. Using their strength/s and weakness/es. From there, you plan an ending that fits the resolution of this character arc, ties all your threads together, and hopefully, satisfies the reader.
- As author Mark Dawson says: "It's like driving at night, where the headlights show you just as much as you need to forge ahead. Any time you get stuck, consider what the hero wants and what they're doing to get it."

CRAFTING YOUR STORY

- Define your main conflict – what is the big story question?
- Who is the protagonist?
- From which point of view are you writing?
  - First person – I am the narrator
  - Second person – you are the narrator (rare)
  - Third person, limited – he/she is the narrator, and only their perspective shows
  - Third person, omniscient – he/she is the narrator, but he/she knows everyone's thoughts
- What does your protagonist want and why?
- In what situation do they start?
- What changes to start their journey now?
- Mini-goals – create mini-goals that are needed to get to the big story goal
  - What is the goal?
  - What complicates the task?
  - How will they overcome the task?
  - Does that make it worse?
  - (Repeat above several times)
- In what situation do they finish?

Example: Restless farm boy (situation) Luke Skywalker (protagonist) wants nothing more than to leave home and become a starfighter pilot, so he can live up to his mysterious father (objective). But when his aunt and uncle are murdered (disaster) after purchasing renegade droids, Luke must free the droids' beautiful owner and discover a way to stop (conflict) the evil Empire (opponent) and its apocalyptic Death Star.

STEP BY STEP

- Introduce your key character(s), usually in a daily life event, but with a conflict.
- Introduce your main story arc (character's main goal).
- Introduce subplots adding to or supplementing your main story arc.
- Throw crap at your main character as they moves toward their goal.
- Bonus points for making things more difficult with the main character's poor decisions.
- Make things worse, and worse again, before they can be better.
- One of the best pieces of advice I ever read about creating conflict is to ask yourself, "What's the worst thing that could happen to my character right now?" Find something that answers this question and fits within your world, and you have created tense, interesting, high-conflict scenes that drive the plot.
- Make sure the win is due to the main character's agency (ability to act). It takes a true master to make a "hand of God" ending work, and most of us aren't Stephen King writing The Stand. Don't try this at home, kids.

If you're stuck for ideas, some inspiration sources include favorite quotes, themes or issues dear to your heart, or a new take at an existing book theme, such as Wicked does, on the Wizard of Oz.

> Write down your ideas when you get them.

I come up with my best thoughts for plots, characters, subplots, or scenes just as I'm drifting off to sleep. Keep a pad and paper or your phone to make notes, so you don't forget in the morning (spoiler alert: you will). I dictate emails to myself when I get ideas while driving. The biggest lie we can tell ourselves is that we'll remember it later.

What happens if you have too many ideas? Choose the one which inspires you the most right now. Go with your hottest passion at the moment and commit to it. Write the others down in a file (I keep a spreadsheet) to use later, if you want.

I find it very difficult, personally, to work on more than one project at a time as a first draft. It pulls my subconscious attention in too many directions. I can have one in first draft, one in editing, and one in second edits, but not more than one in first draft or I go crazy. I actually descend into this personal hell for the first draft of this book, since I wasn't quite finished with the first draft before November 1, and wanted to start a novel for NaNoWriMo (National Novel Writing Month). I stopped at 90% finished, started the new novel, and then stopped after my 50,000 words were done, and went back to a third round of editing a third book. Once that editing was done and sent off, I could return to finish this draft. The NaNoWriMo novel is still hovering at the back of my head, ½ done and haunting me mercilessly.

SYNOPSIS EXERCISE: Expand your three paragraphs into a 500-700 word synopsis. Give a sentence each to describe your main characters and the major supporting characters. The full synopsis should include subplots, side characters, motivations, goals, barriers, and three strong climaxes, each one bigger than the last. These end in the third and final climax scene and the denouement.

Sometimes I go crazy and end up with a 3,000-word synopsis, but that was a special case for a book with six points of view.

At this point, I have to take a break. My head is swimming with possibilities, and the scenes are already forming in my head. No! Not yet! Back, back you fools! You're not in queue yet. I need my characters first.

CHAPTER FIVE:
CHARACTER DEEP DIVE

Finally, it's time to dive deep into the characters.

The main character, also known as the protagonist, is always the toughest to create. They are also the most important to get right. They set the theme for the whole book. You will want your readers to identify with them, root for them, cry when they are hurt, feel triumphant when they persevere and win in the end.

To make this happen, that character must be three-dimensional. They should not be a "Mary Sue," a character that has too many good characteristics without balancing flaws. If you are unsure if your character qualifies, there are online "Mary Sue tests" you can take to verify.

I plan my characters out in a manner similar to creating a character in a role-playing game like Dungeons & Dragons.

NAMES

Now, the character will need many things, starting with a name. Some authors love to create meaningful, significant names. Others are satisfied with something that sounds cool. I try to balance the two, with the added difficulty of using authentic names of the time period and place I'm writing in.

Since my novels are mostly set in Ireland, I give my characters Irish names, and American audiences are unused to the spelling and pronunciations. I try to find names in the records of the time that are easily pronounced and "sound" Irish. Orlagh, Donal, Cormac, names like that.

I try to avoid vanilla names, like Mary, Jane, Tom, Joe, etc. You want your readers to remember the characters, and common names slide off the memory like butter off a hot knife. You want these names to stick like peanut butter!

Gratuitous punctuation common to many fantasy novels can also be bad. If you write fantasy, please don't fall into the trap of making your names so unusual and alien that no one bothers learning it. Many readers will just skip over an odd name and get confused, especially if there are too many difficult ones. Names like T'f-kaLand-er3 will make readers just skip it.

MOTIVATION/GOALS

After you name them, they must have a motivation, a purpose that drives them through the story and conflict. That may or may not be the same as their goal. A person might be motivated by love, yet their goal is to have a family. They might be driven by revenge, but their goal is to get the bad guy arrested. They might act from desperation, but their goal is to survive. Goals are usually more immediate, one-time occurrences, while motivation is an underlying drive.

Not all goals have to be overarching, either! In fact, every scene should have a goal for the character. It might be to get a glass of ice water. It might be to brush their hair or drive to work. Things get in the way of that goal. This makes conflict, which is far more interesting to read about than everything going peachy-keen. Yes, I just said peachy-keen. Deal with it.

CONFLICT

Once your motivations and goals are set, time to bring in some conflict. Internal conflict can be mental challenges, torn loyalties, personal insecurities. External conflicts can be anything from office drama to worldwide war.

Let me say this loud for those in the back.

> There is no good story without good conflict.

DESCRIPTION

You might want to get into the physical description of your character now. How old are they? Short? Tall? Do they have a gender? Hair color? Eyes? A hitched shoulder from a football injury? A limp? Blind? You don't have to get into great detail in the story (and better if you don't infodump it all!) but it should be in your mind as the author and drop hints now and then.

What does your character like to do? Do they have a pet? Do they like cooking? Making swords? Conjuring up demons from the depths of hell? Do they do these things well, or are they a screw-up? Do they have favorite phrases they like to say, especially when upset? Curses are a great way to build a character's uniqueness.

I have a bad tendency to polarize my characters, especially the female leads. They end up being either contrary and sniping or passive and weak. I'm definitely going with the former for Grandma here, but I hope to make her kind as well. But with a nasty temper and a tendency to rap people hard with her walking stick. Because why not?

I fill in her physical characteristics, her hobbies, her quirks. Tics and habits. Catch phrases, favorite curses, anything to humanize her. Does she like cloud-watching? Play with her hair? Yell "Gadzooks!" when she meets someone new?

Once you've built up a nice, strong character profile for your main character, with several paragraphs of details on their personality, appearance, and goals, do the same for the antagonist. Yes, they should be just as three-dimensional as the protagonist. Each antagonist is a hero in their own mind.

> **ANTAGONIST EXERCISE:** Write up a description of your antagonist, including physical description, some backstory, pet phrases, goals, and stakes.

You should have a good collection of people from your synopsis at this point. I've got a dozen in mine at this point, including Irish, Normans, Norsemen, and some Fae.

Make some inflexible, some easy-going. Don't go for the obvious. Make the churchman the easy-going one and the Fool the guy with a stick up his butt. Mix it up. Find those flaws and good points. No one is a perfect villain or a perfect hero in real life, and vanilla, one-dimensional characters make stories boring. Make sure each of your characters has motivations, and for the bigger ones, good story arcs and growth within the story. The walk-on characters don't need it to the same extent as the protagonist, but at least a motivation, virtues and flaws, and some physical characteristics.

Once the characters are fleshed out, go back to your synopsis and re-read it. Do the motivations and goals make sense for the plot points? If not, adjust either character sheets or the synopsis. Make refinements. Add another subplot or combine a few. Maybe you need more characters to make it work? Adjust and revise as needed.

Now, it's time to leave this project for a while. I'm going back to editing an earlier manuscript. That gives me time to let the synopsis, characters, and scenes percolate in my brain while my palate clears.

CHAPTER SIX:
SETTING THE SCENE... LIST

WIP – Work in Progress. This describes the project you're working on, started but not finished. It can be a novel, a poem, a short story, any creative thing.

This is where my inner accountant shines. I create my scene list in a spreadsheet. If you are a crazy person and don't adore spreadsheets for the magical tool they are, I understand some people work well with Scrivener, where you can put in a description of the scene as the title. Making a list in Word works for others. Either way, an Extreme Planner should make a list. It really helps.

Why does it help? I am so glad you asked. I shall delight in telling you.

When you have limited time to write each day, as most of us do, you will want to maximize that time the best way you can. If you have a comprehensive scene list written out, while you're writing in a scene, you know where the scene needs to end up to be ready for the next scene.

Remember that synopsis you wrote? Pull that out. Read it once again to ensure it still flows and makes sense. You might have thought of some refinements since you created it. Add those in.

Now, I take my synopsis and create a blow-by-blow list of scenes. Each scene has a basic description of what happens. For instance, my opening scene is "Orlagh gives her chief a prophecy of an incoming Norman invasion. He doesn't believe her." This sets scene, which characters are present, and a basic conflict within the scene. That's it. Scene One described.

Go through your synopsis to write scene after scene. The reason I love the spreadsheet is because it's easy to insert/delete lines to shift things around if they make better sense to the story flow. I will expand my story line as I get deeper into the details of the plot and add to my synopsis as I go.

Some people enjoy using software like Scrivener for this portion. I've tried Scrivener, and it works fine, but I prefer Excel. Scrivener has issues with destroying formatting that I find annoying. But it works for others, and it is easier to move the entire scenes around when you can find them more easily. Use the tools which work best with your own flow habits.

As the scene list is created, it ebbs and flows, in conjunction with the synopsis. This, to me, is the most creative part of the planning.

NOVEL SIZE

- Novelette (7,500-17,500 words)
- Novella (17,500-40,000 words)
- Novel (40,000-120,000 words)
- Supernovel (120,000+ words)

Some genres have a common word count range. These are the standard ranges you most often see bandied around for adult commercial and literary fiction:

- Below 70,000: Too short
- 70,000 – 79,999: Might be too short; probably all right
- 80,000 – 89,999: Totally cool
- 90,000 – 99,999: Generally safe
- 100,000 – 109,999: Might be too long; probably all right
- 110,000 or above Too long

Now, despite all the above constraints, the first draft does not need to be within those ranges. Lots happens during the editing process, so write your first draft as long as it needs to be to tell the story. Worry about market constraints later.

For instance, romance novels tend to be around 50K-70K words, while epic fantasies tend to be over 100K due to all the world-building. Chick lit tends to be about 70-75K.

SCENES

I like to picture my scenes like a movie in my head, blocking out who is where, what they're doing, what the area around them looks, smells, and sounds like. Who is angry? Who is depressed? What weapons are coming at the main character's back? Why are there chickens? Who brought the muffins?

Essential elements
- Conflict – easy lives are boring. Give us war, anger, disaster, strife, arguments. This makes for intriguing storylines.
- Story arc – Your story should have a beginning, middle, and end, and a growth along that curve.
- Character arc – So should your main characters. The ending personality should have learned something along the way.
- Character-driven elements – in-depth characters with internal conflicts and inner growth
- Action-driven story elements – Usually action-packed stories, lots of external conflicts that force your character to react.
- Subplots – "side jobs," such as the supporting character's love pursuit, the main character's problem with their second son, or the annoying landlord in the background. They add color and depth to the story. Also, in real life, nothing happens in a vacuum. Every person has a multitude of stresses pulling them in all directions. Think of your personal stressors, such as work, school, family, societal expectations, finances, ideals. Each one of those pulls on you, and is your own personal subplot.

- Theme – A basic premise behind the story, for example, betrayal, love, mystery, death, renewal, isolation, jealousy, lust, power, survival, spirituality, etc.
- Tone – A horror story will have a very different tone from a cozy mystery, even though they both deal with a crime.
- Pacing - try to balance these three main elements:
  - Dialogue (too much is exhausting)
  - Action (again, exhausting. Needs rest between)
  - Narrative (too much is boring)

A secret: Keeping your synopsis up to date will be a boon later, when an agent asks for a synopsis of your story.

I add a timeline to my scene list (again, on a spreadsheet, because I love spreadsheets. They are my precious). You can also use the spreadsheet to keep track of your themes and subplots.

SCENE EXERCISE: Write a list of your three highest-conflict scenes.

As you can see in the below example, I have brief descriptions of my scenes, details such as whose point of view the scene is in, as well as where and when it is.

After I get the scenes listed out, I spend time rearranging them, balancing character point of views, action, and the high-energy scenes vs. low-energy scenes. Then I color code them. I highlight the highest-conflict scenes in red, those that represent the three climaxes in the three-act structure. Then I do the next highest in orange, and lower conflict scenes in yellow. The "rest/recover" scenes get green. Again, this provides a visual way of judging the pace of your novel.

Scene	POV	Date
Orla overhears Malachi talking to the chief about her being a witch on Twelfth Night	Orla	9-Jan
She goes to her herb room and gets out her frustrations on the herbs - and takes a drink to calm herself	Orla	9-Jan
At dinner, chief is dicussing his plans for the new abbey, with the Bishop on his side. Arguments. Money.	Orla	10-Jan
Declan getting fired from his farm job	Declan	10-Jan
Declan traveling on the road, hungry. Stealing to survive. He signs for his supper at a tavern.	Declan	12-Jan
Passing Ostmen don't like the songs, but hires him. The work is nasty, but he takes it. Strangr-fjordr	Declan	13-Jan
The chief summons her to prophesy for him. The vision is dark, so she hedges it.	Orla	13-Jan
Flashback to when she received the brooch from her grandfather	Orla	Past
Encounter with an angry Bishop Malachi in the market	Orla	15-Jan
Declan doing hated scut work. He sings off on his own. Meets Hellevi, a free camp follower. She loves his singing.	Declan	16-Jan
Declan learns basics of smithing from Trygve to impress Hellevi	Declan	17-Jan
Encounter with Hellevi and Trygve. Declan vows to protect her from the smith.	Declan	17-Jan

I also keep a running total of my word count. I enter my cumulative word count every day (easily seen in a Word document) and it calculates what that day's count is and then the weekly count. I set myself a 2000 word a day minimum and usually make it. Sometimes not, but I don't beat myself up about it. If I make my weekly goal, I'm happy.

Cumulative Word Count	Daily Word Count	Weekly Word Count	Date
1,870	1,870		23-Aug
3,877	2,007		24-Aug
7,260	3,383		25-Aug
7,260	-		26-Aug
9,409	2,149		27-Aug
9,409	-		28-Aug
10,981	1,572	10,981	29-Aug
15,225	4,244		30-Aug
17,147	1,922		31-Aug

Remember that this scene list is a guide, not a jail. It is designed to help keep you on a path, but that path is not a highway. It's a rambling forest path with side paths and places where you might have to forge your own way. It's organic, malleable, and to be used as a tool, not a mandate.

> **SCENE LIST EXERCISE:** Expand your scene list to include subplots and bridge scenes between the high-conflict scenes.

I end up with about 70-80 scenes for an 80,000-word manuscript. Because I delight in statistics, my scene length usually ends up around 1,000-1,100 words. I consider that to be on the short side, so whenever I go over that amount, I'm happier. However, we're still creating the scene list, so I'll come back to that later.

If you are writing the manuscript from more than one point of view, I add a column to my spreadsheet indicating POV, so I can visually see if the distribution is too overbalanced. This was critical in my latest WIP, Taming of the Few. I have no less than six point-of-view protagonists. This prospect, once I conceived of it, scared the hell out of me. But with my handy-dandy spreadsheet, it worked out in the end. I hope. See, more Extreme Planning! It hasn't been published yet as of this writing, so whether it worked or not is yet to be determined.

I might do some more spot-research here and there, add a few more subplots, side characters, or maybe combine a few. It takes a few drafts for me to figure out all the convolutions.

I wrote up my scene list with point of view, timeline, and places. First were the scenes, then I placed them via a map. Then I researched the dates the background historical events took place, to make sure I anchored my pivotal scenes around these events. I also had to make sure the dates worked with the places (i.e., if I'm in Ballynoe one day, I can't be in Emain Macha the next because my main character is a 65-year-old grandmother and can't travel 50 miles in a day. Maybe three days, even with a fresh horse). The whole book will take place during a month, From mid-January to mid-February, 1177 CE.

I had seventy scenes listed at first. That number is not set in stone, of course. I'll add scenes, combine them, and expand the basic plot. It's so much easier writing a scene list with a good 3-page synopsis to work from.

I have two points of view in this novel. The Main Character (Orlagh) and her adult grandson (Declan). I listed all her scenes first, then all his. I then interspersed them appropriately for how it made the most sense. And for maximum tension. It's like shuffling cards.

Especially for when he gets offered as sacrifice to the Norse Gods.

And I have a gift for my patient readers at the end. This is the first book in the series where we get a peek into the world of the Faeries. In the end, someone actually travels there and sees what's to be their home for the rest of their days. That will be fun to describe, and that fun will be my own reward for getting to the end of the first draft. Each subsequent book will take place more and more inside the Faerie world.

This step took me only about an hour and a half to do. However, if I hadn't had my synopsis and character list already set, I have no idea how long it would be. Much longer.

My next step will be to actually, finally, start writing the story. I start with Chapter one, page one. I've written the first couple of lines, as I dreamt of them the other night. That's when I knew I needed to start writing the book soon, or the scenes would start bubbling up in my mind and disperse before I got them all down!

ORGANIZATION EXERCISE: Re-organize your scene list to balance them between high and low conflict, point-of-view characters, and the structure as a whole as per your synopsis. Color code them, and enjoy the beauty of Extreme Planning in all its glory.

CHAPTER SEVEN: OPENING SCENE

The purpose of the opening scene is to hook your readers.

We all know this, in theory. However, execution is often not only difficult to create, almost impossible to perfect, and sometimes so terrifying, we freeze.

Many novels have never been started because the author can't think of a perfect opening scene.

My trick for the Extreme Planner: Don't write an opening scene. Or rather, write an opening scene with every intention of changing it later. The plan is to put a placeholder now, as you concentrate on writing the novel, and getting the initial rounds of editing done. You may do a lot of revision and moving things around as the result of feedback you get from your beta readers and developmental editors. So why worry now about what that perfect first scene will be? You don't know it yet.

Just writing [Insert opening scene here] can help you get over the hump of needing to write it first.

> **FIRST SCENE EXERCISE:** Write the first scene you want, without regard to how exciting or interesting it is. Include all the world-building and character description you want. Put it away for later. Maybe save it as a give-away to your newsletter fans someday.

As I mentioned before, the initial opening scene is often better if cut from the final manuscript. Many writers include way too much backstory or setting in that opening scene. It's often filled with cumbersome exposition and description. Dump it. Cut it. Set it on fire. No, wait! Save it in a file for cut scenes. You may need some of that data later, but it's much more digestible if cut into little bits and fed throughout the story.

This is especially true if your character's back story includes some tragedy. Why would you give that juicy detail away to the reader straight out of the gate? Hint at the tragic tale near the beginning, and dole out breadcrumbs throughout the story, making that tragedy color the character's actions. Make the reader want to get to the end to find out the true details of that mysterious past.

Think of the juicy backstory as spices. Everyone loves a well-spiced meal! But if you pile on too much spice at once, it's unpalatable. A little goes a long way. A sprinkle at the beginning, a bit over here, over there, more in the middle, etc.

As an extreme planner, I like to write infodump scenes just to get it out of my system. Then I cut it out of the main manuscript, working the details in where needed/appropriate. Sometimes it doesn't all make it in on the first draft, or ever. But, for me, it's a lot easier to craft a dynamic scene if I'm not trying to world build at the same time.

> A good first scene, in this modern reader world, usually needs some conflict.

I recommend a "typical life" setting for your main character, and then toss in some chaos. Show their character by how they react to that chaos, rather than telling your reader "She was a sarcastic grandmother" or "He was a hard-edged old soldier." Show the readers by having them argue with someone who is giving them a hard time.

This opening conflict doesn't have to be related to the overarching goal or quest of the character. However, bonus points if you can get it related to either, or to something they've always wanted and can't get.

> The opening scene should create some sense of tension, a fight, an argument, a struggle. It shows the character's mettle and personality far more than descriptive narrative will.

OPENING LINES

You only have one chance to make a great first impression. That is true of novels as well as meeting people.

Fascinating that "opening lines" isn't until halfway through the book, isn't it?

But in my process, there's a lot of work that needs to be done before I can allow myself the torture and luxury that is crafting the opening lines of a novel. There are other methods, of course, but this is my method.

Opening lines are incredibly important. They are the hook that draw your reader into the world you have created. Get them wrong, and your reader may decide to move on. Get them right and you have pure gold.

Don't let this scare you! If need be, start writing your novel with scene two. Or as I suggested earlier, write a placeholder scene, and come back to it. Do whatever trick you can to psych yourself out of paralytic fear and write.

There are many rules to writing but do keep in mind that rules are meant to be broken. If done right, you can get away with breaking them all. But for most mortals, it is good to keep the following in mind.

- **Trope** – in storytelling terms, a common cliché or convention. All genres have tropes associated with them.

Tropes can be used in your story to keep fans of the genre interested. This is called writing to the genre. For instance, romance stories have tropes like enemies-to-lovers and happily ever after endings.

Opening your story with tropes, however, can be dangerous. For instance, the main character wakes from a dream. Or glances at themselves in a mirror, giving the author a chance to describe them. Opening a thriller novel with a thunderstorm. These are tired tropes because they're so overdone. Most agents will automatically reject a book starting with them.

It's not strictly forbidden to use tropes to open your story, but they work best if you add a twist.

> Start with something happening, even if it's just the character wanting a glass of water.

This doesn't have to be ninja-attacking action. It can be an argument. Catch them with some action. It might be something as simple as a phone call or overhearing a co-worker gossip about you. Still, the first scene should have something interesting/exciting going on to draw the reader in.

A term for starting in the middle of the action is in media res, or in the midst of the plot. An example of this is The Odyssey, which starts with most of Odysseus' journey already complete, and only flashes back to what's happened earlier.

On the other hand, don't start in the middle of too much action. You don't want to confuse the poor reader with a ten-person ninja battle before you give them a chance to care for your character. They might not even realize who that character is yet.

Which brings me to my next point. Name your character quickly. I would suggest the first three lines, if not the first. It doesn't have to be his full title and associations. You don't have to mention his name is Chief Ruaidrí mac Con Ulad Mac Duinn Sléibe. You could just say Chief Ruaidrí, or simply the Chief. But give the character a name, perhaps a bit of his personality, right away. Don't keep him as a nebulous blob. Not naming him is distancing, and the reader doesn't connect with them.

This is particularly true if you have dialogue as your opening line. Tell us who is talking right away! Too many unreferred pronouns can easily confuse. It's perfectly clear in your mind's eye, but new readers are a blank slate.

Avoid long exposition or scenery, also known as a data dump. Exposition is lovely and needful, but in small doses. The opening scene of a book is especially vulnerable to such things. One line at a time, interspersed in the action or dialogue, is much more palatable. Yes, I know you want to open the door into your lush and imaginative world. Baby steps!

After you've written a first draft of your novel, take some time to craft killer first lines. Something that people will want to read on to learn more. This is harder than you think! You can brainstorm dozens of lines and still not have a fantastic one. However, the first line has one job – hook the reader. This can be done in a variety of ways, but if you can set up tension, introduce an intriguing concept, or introduce the main character, you're halfway there.

If you decide to start with a bit of philosophy, make sure it segues into your story nicely and fairly quickly. Many classic novels start out this way, and that's wonderful. See below examples, such as Pride and Prejudice. But that is no longer the "popular style," so if you are going to try to make that work, make sure it's flawless. Keep in mind also that many older novelists, like Charles Dickens, wrote in serial form, and were paid by the word. They literally lost money if they wrote too concisely.

Match your sentence length to the action. If there is a fire, use short, choppy sentences to increase tension and immediacy. If the action is a gate crasher at a Victorian tea party, you can use longer sentences to match the more relaxed setting.

It's tempting to be mysterious and flowery in the opening lines. If this is epic fantasy, even more so. But too much mystery can be off-putting as well. Each "unknown" is stored in a reader's brain as something to discover. There are only so many unknowns a reader is willing to hold onto until they are bored and tosses the book at the wall. Choose your mysteries well and make them relevant to the story.

The opening of The Lovely Bones is a great example of this. "My name was Salmon, like the fish; first name Susie. I was fourteen when I was murdered on December 6, 1973."

Right away, you know the main character was murdered. But who murdered her? That's the mystery we search for throughout the book. She doesn't waste time with descriptions yet, but you already know a lot about her.

Make us care for the main character right away. Give us some details about them. Are they avoiding sweets because it will make them fat? Are they worried about the boss's new favorite employee taking over? Are they hung over because their girlfriend dumped them for their best friend?

Try to only introduce two or three characters in the opening scene. Readers are just meeting these people, so it's better to let the reader get to know them a little before bringing in new players. This lets them form an image in their mind and develop sympathy for them.

"It was a Dark and Stormy Night." Don't start with the weather. It's trite, overdone, and pretty boring. Unless your characters are about to be hit by a hurricane or a tsunami, of course.

Yes, those are a lot of rules. There are many others. You can certainly break them, but it's more effective when you learn the rules and how best to break them before you do so. Picasso was excellent at figure drawing before he shifted to breaking the rules with Cubism.

> There are several elements of an opening scene, including the inciting incident, a novel-sized problem, an immediate problem, a setup for the next scene.

You might include some back story, but be cautious. You have limited real estate to get the essential information to your reader. You can introduce several elements, such as the theme, the language, the setting/time, and maybe even hint at issues in the rest of the novel. It's a tall order.

Even if you are looser with your later scenes, make sure that opening scene has definite structure. Beginning, middle, and closure. The purpose of any scene is to give essential information to the reader and to make the reader want more. The opening scene must do all that.

FIRST THREE LINES EXERCISE: Write the first three lines of your scene. Introduce your character, give them an action, give them a conflict. Rewrite until you have all three.

The above seems crippling and scary. There is so much to remember, and so much is riding on these opening lines. So how do I start? What does an Extreme Planner do?

I am aware that not everyone works like this, but I start with a movie in my mind. Others might hear a story in their head. Or flashes of characters or settings. It all depends on how your own mind works. If the movie hasn't happened yet at this point, I do the following.

I pick a scene already in my manuscript. For instance, Misfortune of Vision, is set in 12th century Ireland. I know that the main character, a 65-year-old prophetess, employed by her chief, is going to clash with the new Bishop. So, I decided that the opening scene should be of her walking by the chief's chambers and overhearing the Bishop discuss her.

This is what I've got for now.

January 5th, 1177AD
Dún Dá Leathghlas (Downpatrick), Ulster, Ireland

"She's a witch, Rí Ulad."
Orlagh stopped dead in her tracks. She wasn't in the habit of listening to the Chief's conversations, but the stranger must be speaking of her. The fact that the speaker used the formal title of the Chief of the Ulaidh meant he was someone important. She hadn't learned how to survive in this wicked world by ignoring potential threats. She pressed her ear against the solid oak door. A rustle in the thatch above distracted her, but it was only a rat coming in from the cold.

So, I've got the main character named, the speaker at least described as a stranger to her, and her voice hinted at. She's a strong woman and she knows how to survive. I've established she has some relation to the Chief, and that she is in a structure with a thatched roof and an oak door. Since I've named the date and the town beforehand, that helps fill in the details of setting, even for readers without a firm grasp of what twelfth century life was like in Ireland.

Now I delve into the conversation she overhears between her Chief and the stranger (the Bishop who hates her) and set up the conflict.

Repeat this over and over as you write your first scene.

> You will rewrite your first scene. Many times.
> You will rewrite your first couple of lines. Many times.
> Don't delete them – save them. They may help later.

Maybe five times, maybe fifty times. Get used to that notion. Understand it from the beginning. Don't let the above deter or frighten you. Get something down to start with and know you will come back to it, and you can edit later to your heart's content.

Here are more examples of first lines from classic books that have stood the test of time. Keep in mind some of these break the above rules. While some start with conflict, for instance (Fahrenheit 451, Orlando or The Stranger), many do not. Also remember that popular fiction changes over time, so what worked in the 1950s won't work as well with today's reading audience.

> **FIRST LINE EXERCISE:** Pick two of the below opening lines or one of your own from a well-known novel. How do they use the rules? How do they subvert them? How many elements do they pack into the first line? What questions do they form for the reader?

Read each of these lines and determine how they impact and intrigue you with just a few words. What is done right? What falls flat to you?

- "It was a bright cold day in April, and the clocks were striking thirteen." – 1984
    - Right away, you know the world is different, as we don't have a thirteen on our clocks, outside of the military, and their terminology is different.
- "It is a truth universally acknowledged that a single man in possession of a good fortune must be in want of a wife." – Pride and Prejudice
    - Opening with a bit of philosophy was on brand for Jane Austen, and this theme permeates her entire novel. It works as a perfect tagline.
- "Happy families are all alike; every unhappy family is unhappy in its own way." – Anna Karenina
    - This intriguing bit of philosophy draws interest, as we now expect to be told of an unhappy family, and we aren't disappointed. It makes the reader ask questions.

- "Ships at a distance have every man's wish on board." – *Their Eyes Were Watching God*
  - I love the imagery of this and the allegory of wishes. It promises someone reaching for their dreams.
- "Call me Ishmael." – *Moby Dick*
  - Short, abrupt, and includes the narrator's name. It's an unusual name, and you know right away it's a first-person point of view.
- "Many years later, as he faced the firing squad, Colonel Aureliano Buendía was to remember that distant afternoon when his father took him to discover ice." – *One Hundred Years of Solitude*
  - This sets up the frame tale, introduces conflict and character immediately, and even hints at their back story, lots of heavy lifting for one sentence.
- "It was a pleasure to burn." – *Fahrenheit 451*
  - Again, full of intrigue and questions. What are they burning? Why? To whom was it a pleasure?
- "It was the best of times, it was the worst of times, it was the age of wisdom, it was the age of foolishness, it was the epoch of belief, it was the epoch of incredulity, it was the season of Light, it was the season of Darkness, it was the spring of hope, it was the winter of despair." – *A Tale of Two Cities*
  - This is way too ponderous for modern novels, but it worked well for Dickens. It gives a sweeping setting, highlighting the conflict of war and repression.

- "Someone must have slandered Josef K., for one morning, without having done anything truly wrong, he was arrested." – The Trial
    - Instant conflict, and a mystery about why the conflict occurred. And while we don't know the narrator's name, they tell us about Josef.
- "If you really want to hear about it, the first thing you'll probably want to know is where I was born, and what my lousy childhood was like, and how my parents were occupied and all before they had me, and all that David Copperfield kind of crap, but I don't feel like going into it, if you want to know the truth" – The Catcher in the Rye
    - This opening line is full of the personal voice of the narrator, and not only tells us it's a young adult novel, but that the narrator is telling their own story.
- "It was a wrong number that started it, the telephone ringing three times in the dead of night, and the voice on the other end asking for someone he was not." – City of Glass
    - Conflict and mystery straight out of the gate.
- "Mother died today." – The Stranger
    - Another blunt, strong conflict opening.
- "Dr. Weiss, at forty, knew that her life had been ruined by literature." – The Debut
    - This begs many questions and introduces the character. We might find it difficult to picture how someone's life can be ruined by literature, so we're intrigued and want to read on to discover how it's possible.

- "There was a boy called Eustace Clarence Scrubb, and he almost deserved it." – The Voyage of the Dawn Treader
    - Character introduction, and narrator's voice is snarky. Also, a hint at Eustace's character, which is intriguing. Why does he deserve it?

OPENING SCENE EXERCISE: Write your first scene again, with attention to the above advice, using your first three lines.

PART TWO: THE FIRST DRAFT

CHAPTER EIGHT: THE FRIGHTENING BLANK PAGE

FIRST SCENE (A reiteration of the last chapter)

A hint for the first scene: start with a small conflict. While authors in the past have been able to write classics without this, modern readers are more inclined to want to be drawn in instantly. That means no infodumping of the family history before you introduce the main character, no lengthy back story of the world and its political structure.

Instead, introduce your character right away, with the briefest of descriptions, and drop them into a conflict. It can be small, like an argument, or frustration with a computer program, or a dropped coffee mug. Anything to bring the reader into direct sympathy with the character and show their mettle.

Typically, this allows the reader to identify with the character. While some authors have famously started books with someone other than the main character (I'm looking at you, George R.R. Martin!), this is difficult and requires high skill. He also received a lot of slack for it.

If you are going to pull a GRRM and kill off your main character in your story, you had better do it well. This is a classic case of "First learn the rules and why they are important, then learn how to break them properly." Pablo Picasso was an amazing realistic artist before he dove into his other forms. Same with Salvador Dali.

Another note about the first scene. It doesn't have to be perfect. On a first draft, it doesn't even have to be good. If you are like most authors, you'll likely rewrite, change, shift around, or completely scrap the first scene in subsequent drafts.

"Every first draft is perfect, because all a first draft has to do is exist." – Jane Smiley

If you insist on getting it perfect the first time, you'll never finish the rest of the draft. That is true of both the writing phase and the planning phase.

Another typical thing I've seen, especially with first-time novelists, is that their book is often made stronger by chopping off the first chapter. Or more. My first published novel, Legacy of Hunger, I chopped off the first four chapters. And I likely could have gotten away with more and still not damaged the narrative. Most of that was backstory I included in snippets throughout the rest of the book.

NEXT SCENES

> The goal of the first chapter (and indeed, each subsequent chapter) is to entice the reader to get to the next chapter. In addition, each chapter should provide information on the narrative, character, or setting. Ideally, some of each. It should either move the plot forward or provide vital data.

As I write each scene (from my scene list), I know where I came from (the previous scene) and I know where I need to end up (the next scene) so all I'm really concentrating on is how to bridge that tiny distance between.

This. This is the secret to why extreme planning can make your writing time more efficient. You aren't worrying about how the novel is going to end. You already know that. You aren't worrying about backing your character into a corner you don't know how to rescue them from. You are only worrying about how to get them through this one scene. The amount of uncertainty has been removed from your already overburdened mental shoulders.

In between writing sessions, I think about my next scene, either consciously or unconsciously. It percolates and simmers and bubbles up with ideas and images. Because I know what my next scene is (thanks to my handy-dandy scene list) I know what comes next in the story. I imagine the scene in my head, blocked out like a play or a movie scene. This is pre-writing, coming up with the details before I have my hands on the keyboard. That way, when I do get the time to write, the words fly from my fingertips as fast as I can type them, and I don't waste precious writing time struggling to create the scene details.

Eat that huge elephant one little bite at a time.

Now, things happen as you write. One scene may not be big enough to encompass all that's happening, despite the one-sentence description. You may realize that you must expand that into two, five, or even eight scenes. It happened to me, especially around the climax scenes.

You may also decide that those three scenes are better combined into one, and still cover all the cogent points.

A wild side character can (and often does) pop out of nowhere and take over the narrative for a while. This happens to me often, and some of my favorite characters show up like this. Adhna is one such character in my Druid's Brooch Series. I didn't plan on a dotty old Fae to be the main character's helper and friend. It just happened. They showed up, elbowed their way into the storyline, and stayed for the next six books.

For those pantsers afraid of planning stifling your creativity, rest assured that there are still plenty of ways for that to shine through as you write your scenes.

During this process, you will want to shift your scenes around to fit the new information you find while writing. That's fine. That's why I have it in a spreadsheet. I don't update the synopsis until the end, though, when everything is clearer.

I highlight each scene in my spreadsheet as I finish writing it. I love keeping visual track of my progress. Because I'm an Extreme Planner.

I calculate my percentage of completion, as well. I take my number of scenes planned (80) and divide it by the number of scenes written so far (say, 20). That means I'm 25% through writing the novel. Then I divide my total word count by that percentage, and it gives me an estimate of how many words my novel should end up being. This is a very rough calculation, and it changes as I write either longer or shorter than normal scenes. It changes if I add or subtract scenes as I'm writing. But it keeps me on target to where I want the novel to be.

Usually, I say that a story is as long as it needs to be. If your tale is told in 40,000 words, you have a novella. If it's 80,000, you have a novel. However, when you're writing in a series, it's a good idea to keep your word counts roughly even for consistency, so I set targets. Not that I was great at staying in those targets. My Druid's Brooch Series had some books at 80,000 words, and some at 120,000 words. But the stories all worked well enough.

This is where I'd normally have an exercise for you to work out. However, you've already done the scary part of writing. You have the first chapter written, re-written, and a plan with structure for the rest of your novel. Write to your heart's content!

CHAPTER NINE:
DIALOGUE VS. NARRATIVE VS. ACTION

Dialogue. Narrative. Action.

A well-balanced story has all three elements. In fact, a well-balanced scene should have all three elements, though one may dominate. Too much dialogue can become exhausting. Too much narrative can be boring and cumbersome. Too much action can be overwhelming.

Pace your scenes. If the story is moving too slowly, add some dialogue. If there's too much action, add a reflective/reset scene with some narrative. Are the characters talking too much about things that are better using internal narrative? Are they too much in their heads and need to talk to someone else?

DIALOGUE

Dialogue is how characters develop identity. It's the greatest tool for creating your characters, giving their motivations, fears, and desires. But that's not enough to make the scene scintillate.

Dialogue can be the easiest thing to write, or it can be the most difficult. Sometimes at the same time! Common mistakes are:

- Too formal (though this can be a style choice or a character choice)
- Too realistic (same as above)
- Obtrusive dialogue tags
- Overuse of names or pronouns
- Talking head syndrome
- Homogenous characters
- Explaining the dialogue

TOO FORMAL

We're writers. I get it. We want to use proper grammar. But not all your characters will speak with perfect grammar. People speak in incomplete sentences, colloquialisms, accents, and filler words. They say things like "I literally died!" and "If I was you…" and "Prolly!"

In addition, people don't tend to give long diatribes in complex sentences, because they've usually not worked out the perfect words beforehand, like a good speechwriter does.

TOO REALISTIC

I mentioned filler words above. In real speech, people use words like "uh," "um," "er," "like," etc. constantly, especially those who are searching for the right words or are uncomfortable speaking. While a few of these are fine to emphasize a character's discomfort, don't use as many as they really use.

In addition, let's discuss accents and dialect. Interesting characters can have interesting accents. My advice is to use such things sparingly. Use different words to portray regional accents (like pop vs. soda) and go light on the pronunciation differences ("I'm tellin' ya" vs. "Ahm tellin' ya"). A little goes a long way.

You can also change the order of words according to the native language of the speaker. For instance, articles in Russian are either missing or optional, so many Russians leave them out in English. "I go to house and pick up sister," suggests a Slavic speaker.

Phonetic spellings are another tool of portraying accent or dialect. An example for a French accent might be "Ze corpse was found in ze river zis morning. 'Ow did it get there?" Again, use this tool very sparingly, as it can get ponderous quickly. Making the reader stop and pronounce the word either out loud or subvocal can interrupt the flow. In addition, it can be seen as mocking a region, class, race, or background, so be cautious and respectful.

OBTRUSIVE DIALOGUE TAGS

"I can't see!" John said.

"Well, open your eyes!" Jane said.

"I have – it's still dark." John said.

"Wait, let me turn the light up." Jane said.

As you can see, that's annoying. Most readers will ignore the words "said," but at a certain point, it becomes overwhelming, like above.

"I can't see!" John whined.
"Well, open your eyes!" Jane responded.
"I have – it's still dark." John complained.
"Wait, let me turn the light up." Jane sighed.

A little better, but too contrived. You can tell the author is trying too hard to not use "said." A better approach is to combine action tags and reactions to indicate who is speaking.

John whined, "I can't see!"
Jane crossed her arms. "Well, open your eyes!"
"I have – it's still dark." John's voice rose in panicked confusion.
Jane fumbled with the lamp controls. "Wait, let me turn the light up."

Also, notice how some of the tags are before the speech itself. That lets the reader know who is speaking so the words are colored with that character's voice in their mind. To put it after and make them guess can result in a disconnect in their mental "performance" of the dialogue and interrupt the reader's flow.

OVERUSE OF NAMES OR PRONOUNS
Consider this dialogue:

"Hey, John, what's up?"
"Not much, Jim. Did you finish that project?"

"No, John, I forgot. Sorry!"
"No worries, Jim. I can get it next week."

While the advantage is you don't need dialogue tags, real people don't talk like this. The opposite problem can also be bad:

Jim approached his co-worker, John. "Hey, what's up?"

He glanced at him, noticing his furrowed brow. "Not much. Did you finish that project?"

He shook his head, chucking him on the shoulder. "No, I forgot. Sorry!"

With a smile, he shrugged. "No worries. I can get it next week."

Did you lose track of which he was which? Make certain you don't overuse the pronouns, or make sure it's clear who is who within both the action and the dialogue.

"TALKING HEAD SYNDROME"
"John, where have you been?"
"Oh, just… out."
"Out where?"
"You know, errands. The bank, haircut, library."
"Think you're cute, don't you? Howard called. He said you were playing slots again."

No actions, no narrative, no reactions, just words. Did you lose track of who was speaking? Who is talking TO John? Do we even know their gender? Do you know the setting? Is John making tea? Getting dressed? Petting the dog? Let's try this again.

Tanya crossed her arms, her eyes glittering with annoyance. "John, where have you been?"

After shaking the rain from his coat, John hung it on the peg by the door. "Oh, just… out."

"Out where?"

He shrugged, trying to sound casual, and slid past her toward the kitchen. "You know, errands. The bank, haircut, library."

Narrowing her eyes, Tanya's glare intensified as she stomped after him. "Think you're cute, don't you? Howard called. He said you were playing slots again."

The additions of a few actions, a few elements of the setting, and some narrative of the characters reactions (sounding casual, annoyed, glare intensified) bring this scene to life and give a much better picture of how each character is acting, why, and how their partner is reacting to those actions, above and beyond the words. Body language, subtext, and hidden agendas can now be highlighted.

HOMOGENOUS CHARACTERS

Dialogue is a fantastic tool to differentiate your characters and highlight their personalities, motivations, fears, habits, etc. If all your characters sound the same, the reader may have a hard time keeping them separate in their mind.

Whenever I create a character profile, I note their goals, fears, pet phrases, favorite foods, hobbies, etc., to help color their actions and dialogue, and so each character is distinct.

- One character may curse a lot while another prefers a euphemistic phrase, like "Oh, fudge!"
- Some characters are more eloquent, and some less expressive.
- Politeness levels
- Education levels
- Temper
- Extrovert/introvert
- Teenagers speak with a different rhythm, speed, and slang than elders. "Yeet" vs. "Chuck it"

EXPLAINING THE DIALOGUE

This is when the narrative near the dialogue is explaining to the reader what just happened. If you've done the dialogue and action tag well, usually such explanations are redundant.

Some examples, with the redundant parts highlighted:

"That's unfair! I hate you!" John slammed the door and stormed to his room. He was furious with his best friend.

Carol turned with a sigh to apologize to her husband. "I'm so sorry, Don."

Brian looked into the sky to search for the planet. "I can't see Mars at all. Can you?"

> **DIALOGUE EXERCISE:** Rewrite the below dialogue using the information above. Use action tags and setting details to spice it up.

Mary asked, "Were you hoping to be missed?"
Jack said, "How could I be missed? I was wearing a bright purple plaid leisure suit."
"What if someone was reading instead of watching?"
Jack said, "Their loss, I suppose."
"Well, I would be reading," Mary responded.

NARRATIVE

Narrative isn't just the description behind the dialogue. It can contain several elements, such as plot, setting, characters, point of view, theme, symbolism, and conflict. Each scene can contain some or all of these, as well as dialogue and action. The most effective writers use all three in combination to advance the information needed.

Some examples of narrative tools:

- Passage of time
- "As you know, Bob..."
- Setting up a plot
- Describe setting
- Backstory
- Describe characters
- Inner conflict

PASSAGE OF TIME

Dialogue is immediate, now, and real-time. Narrative can bring the story forward hours, days, even years, with just a few sentences. It can even bring the story backwards, in a flashback or memory. A few hints can do the trick.

- Twelve years later, Tarren couldn't believe she was now the mother of two teenagers.

- Mag thought back to their twelfth birthday, and shuddered. They never wanted to remember that day, but it always intruded on them in times like these.
- The following week, David checked in on his mother, but her room looked absolutely barren.

"AS YOU KNOW, BOB…"

One mistake some writers make is using dialogue when narrative is more suited. For example, one common fallacy is called the "As you know, Bob…" In this, one character explains history or back story to another who already has this data. Both characters know it, so there is no need for the dialogue, but in order to inform readers of this information, the writer includes it. This should be in narrative instead.

"As you know, Alice, my Death Ray depends on the blood of kittens."

"Damn it, Bob, you know full well that Alice hasn't been the same since that tragic kitten incident."

To combat the "As You Know, Bob…" issue, show rather than tell. Yes, I know this contradicts one of the basic truisms of fiction writing, but in some cases, it really is better than to provide information through the narrative rather than in dialogue. This is one of those times.

UNBROKEN NARRATIVE BLOCKS ARE DIFFICULT TO READ

Though this fish, whose loud sonorous breathing, or rather blowing, has furnished a proverb to landsmen, is so well known a denizen of the deep, yet is he not popularly classed among whales. But possessing all the grand distinctive features of the leviathan, most naturalists have recognized him for one. He is of moderate octavo size, varying from fifteen to twenty-five feet in length, and of corresponding dimensions round the waist. – Moby Dick, Herman Melville

While this sort of writing style had been the norm years ago, this is difficult to slog through for modern readers. Unless your stylistic choice is to write in the manner of Dickens, Melville, or Austen, shorter and more concise narrative is more desirable.

SETTING UP A PLOT

Narrative fills in the bits that aren't as suited to dialogue and action, like internal decisions and character observations. Flashbacks, considerations, back story, these are all elements suited to narrative descriptions.

Sara didn't remember much about her mother. She had always smelled of gardenias and had a tinkling laugh. Sara realized she couldn't even remember her mother's face. In a panic, she climbed into the attic and searched for a particular old box. After a few paper cuts and several sneezes, she pulled out the old photo album, wiped off the dust, and opened it, a slow smile crossing her face. The picture of a woman with curly brown hair, a sweet smile, and dark eyes. Sara wondered what really happened to her.

Poignant? Intriguing? That last sentence sets up a mystery. This could be done in dialogue, if someone else were present, but this treatment is more intimate, more personal. This is her private memory, something to be held close and treasured.

DESCRIBE SETTING

One big part of narrative is setting, which is one of my favorite tools. I love creating immersive settings in a cinematic style. I love describing the view, scents, and tactile sensations a character experiences to bring the reader right into the story.

She walked along the forest path, rotting autumn leaves touched with frost crunching under her soft, calfskin boots. Skeletal branches tugged at her cloak as she passed, scratching her cheek with thoughtless menace.

Were you there? Could you feel the branches? Hear the crunching of the leaves? While I combined action with narrative, most of this was narrative-centered. This scene used just a few sentences, but incorporated sight, scent, touch, and sound. Using at least two or three of the senses in each scene setting helps to anchor the reader in place.

> **SENSES EXERCISE:** Think of the last place you went, be it a grocery store, the garage, or a park. Describe it in detail, using yourself as a character. What do you hear? What do you smell? Is the light playing in the leaves? Is the snow crunching under your foot? Is there a murmur of conversation near the cheese section?

BACKSTORY

Including backstory in the opening pages is the same as saying to the reader, "Wait a minute—hold on. Before I tell you the story, first there's something about these characters and this situation that you need to know."

Tolkien could do it – but it takes a master. Also, that style of writing was more popular in his era. Sprinkle that information throughout the book, a tidbit at a time. Imagine your information on backstory is like a piece of candy. Too much at once can make the reader sick to their stomach, so dole them out at judicious times. Make them search for the clues. Make them eager to find the clues, like ET following a line of Reese's Pieces.

Michelle glanced over her manuscript, her lip curling in an expression of disgust. She really hated where she'd left it, but didn't have the strength to dive back in, not after the accident.

What accident? Why did she stop writing? Readers want to know – and telling them right away is too soon. Let them read on to find the answer.

DESCRIBE CHARACTERS

Characters are well described with both action and dialogue, but sometimes narrative is also useful. Again, infodump is a huge danger. Some of the tritest openings of a novel include the main character looking into a mirror and describing what they see. Don't do this! It's so tired, and most agents and publishers will roll their eyes and toss the manuscript upon seeing it, unless there's something so compelling about it that it rises above the cliché.

Lisa always hated her hair. It always managed to catch in her mouth when the wind blew and it never stayed styled once the humidity hit it. Still, she detested short hair styles on tall women. With her blond hair and tan skin, she'd look like a deformed mushroom with a bob cut.

INNER CONFLICT

Internal arguments and conflict are great areas of narrative. When a character needs to make a decision, but has to weigh the pros and cons of each option, unless she has someone she can hash the details out with, internal narrative is the best option.

Mattea really needed to go to work today, but her migraine pounded against her skull like a heavy-metal drummer in a crazed acid frenzy. However, she remembered her mortgage and her mother's medical bills, and shoved herself out of the warm, comfortable bed, cringing as her bare feet touched the cold floorboards.

ACTION

Action is the physical movements a character makes, whether it be picking up a cup of tea or punching another character between the legs. It creates the movement in a story. It makes the novel more than just a bunch of people standing around and talking. Even that can have action – hand gestures, angry expressions, hugs, etc. Action can bring a story to life, and lack of it can remove all vitality. You don't need to blow up a planet or kill a person to have good action. But something has to happen.

Conflict drives story, and action is often a part of conflict, even in cerebral literary tales. Ulysses by James Joyce had the main character walking from place to place as his day went on.

STARTING YOUR STORY WITH ACTION

Common advice is to start your story with action, in media res (in the middle of things). I find that's true, but more accurate to say start your story with conflict. Some sort of tension or struggle that the main character has to solve. It doesn't have to be a major event. It could be a husband and wife having an argument, or a child struggling with their math exam. It's the reader's first view into your world. Give them something to intrigue them.

MAJOR EVENTS VS. COMMON ACTIONS

- Major actions are plot twists, climaxes, battles, inciting events which drive up tension. They are often the result of conflict, decision, etc.
    - Major events can be the call to action or inciting incident (the action that shoves the main character into the story)
    - Mid-story actions might be the second and third major events

> Most stories have at least two to three major events (Acts) through a full-sized novel. However, if yours works with four or five, fantastic. This is a guideline, not a rule!

- - Climax – the final major event which wraps up the major story arc.

- Common actions include gestures, and everyday actions that add color to your characters and plot
  - Physical actions – tiptoeing, fist fights, phone calls, etc.
  - Psychological actions – glances, innuendo, etc.
  - Vary the pattern to keep interest

> Give characters common habits – biting nails, whistling, nervous giggling. This helps differentiate the characters and makes them more three-dimensional.

- - Intersperse the common actions within dialogue and narrative to pepper it, keep it interesting to the reader.
  - Make your action match the environment. Glances between characters are more difficult in the dark, for instance.

BUILDING UP TENSION

Action can be used to build up tension in the story. Imagine someone in a dark house, searching each shadowed corner with a flashlight, looking for the source of the beating heart thundering in their ears. Nothing has really happened, except the character walking, searching, maybe shining their flashlight at a few spots, but the readers can tell this might result in a jump-scare at any moment, so the tension builds.

HIGH PHYSICAL ACTION SCENES

These can be very difficult to visualize, describe, and not every story needs them. However, a good action scene can liven up many stories. Block out each section of the scene with stick figures, like a storyboard. First A is here, and B is over there, but C is watching. Next, A has lunged for B while C tries to intervene. C trips, and B accidentally stabs him with the sword instead of A. Once you have an idea in your head of how it might look in a movie, then you can more easily describe it. Don't describe every detail, but do consult someone experienced in that area of action. Include salient items that help move the action along in the readers' imagination. I know very little of ballet, but if I had a ballet dance in my scene, I'd try to find someone familiar with ballet to get details from or ask them to read my efforts.

Common wisdom has each of these elements, dialogue, action, and narration, around 1/3 of your manuscript. Obviously a high-action novel will skew, as will a very self-examining biopic. However, it's a good rule of thumb to use.

> **FIGHT SCENE EXERCISE:** Choose a fight scene from your favorite action movie. Write it out in narrative style.

CHAPTER TEN: SCENE BY SCENE

There are many ways to create scenes. Some writers just write what they imagine, and trust that it works as part of the larger work. I have to admit, despite being an Extreme Planner, I fall into this bucket. Others pay careful attention to the bones of each scene, and ensure it includes each part. What parts, you wonder? So glad you asked.

WHAT IS A SCENE?

A scene is a self-contained portion of a longer work, such as a book. It's a building block of the novel. They can vary in length, but usually take place in one area, between one or a group of characters. Scenes make up chapters, then chapters make up books.

> Usually, a change of setting means a change of scene.

There are exceptions, of course, but this is the general rule. Think of when a movie cuts to black between one place and another; that's a scene break.

WHAT SHOULD BE IN A SCENE?

While not every scene must have all of these (like the link to the next scene), a good scene contains most of them.

- Some setting or surroundings, be it the kitchen, the edge of a cliff, or on the deck of a spaceship.
- At least one character engaging in something, be it action, internal musings, or dialogue.
- Its own mini-story, with a beginning, a middle, and an end.
- Rising tension or conflict, which can be internal or external, obvious or subtle.
- Move the story or character forward.
- Something should change, be it the character's attitude, knowledge, or the world around them.
- A strong ending. See if cutting the last lines or paragraphs increases the tension in a cliffhanger.
- A link to the next scene.

METHODS OF SCENE CONSTRUCTION

- Scene and Sequel

Scene and sequel is a well-known story-writing technique where each high tension scene is followed by a sequel designed to rest and reset the action of the next high tension scene. The sequel part allows the character to process and react to the prior scene, and to prepare for the next one. It's an effective technique, and I know many authors use it, either intentionally or instinctually. I don't always use it, but I've often found myself following it without realizing.

> Each scene should have a goal, conflict, or disaster.
> Each sequel should have reaction, dilemma, or decision.
> String those together within the larger arc of rising tension to each major conflict.

- Save the Cat!

Save the Cat! Is a book by Blake Snyder on how to write a screenplay using "story beats" or checkpoints. (They also have one on novels now). They boil film plot structure down to fifteen beats, along with suggested page numbers for each beat, into a template authors can use. I'm not personally a fan of this strict format, though I'm sure it works better for screenplays than novels. However, many authors find great value from their suggestions, and use them to their advantage.

PLANNING YOUR SCENE

In order to plan out a scene you want to first identify the purpose of the scene. Is this where you plant a red herring that will throw off your readers, thinking the murderer is someone innocent? Or do your two protagonists meet for the first time? Maybe your sidekick character is severely injured, giving your protagonist a tough decision, to leave them behind or fight for them. The purpose of the scene will set the tone, structure, and details for you.

If you followed the earlier planning, you've already got the purpose of the scene in your handy-dandy spreadsheet. Each one-sentence description should distill the main reason for including the scene. You can add to that with secondary purposes, weaving in subplots and themes, and make the scene fit into the whole in a cohesive manner. However, I usually end up doing things like that on my second draft, as I don't know the entire story yet on my first draft. Yes, even me as an extreme planner, do pantsing during my first draft. I can't help it! Sometimes characters just refuse to do what you planned for them. It often gets messy.

Regardless of your process, if you start with a solid structure, editing is easier.

I like to imagine my scene from the top, as if literally looking down on it. What's the first thing I see? Where my characters are. Are they sitting in a wooded glade around a campfire? In an office filled with cubicles? On an airplane diving toward a mountain? Giving just a sentence or two of setting helps the reader anchor themselves into place and time. It also helps set the mood.

Don't bludgeon the reader with descriptions, though. While a few salient points literally set the scene, three paragraphs on the shade of blue for the curtains will make your readers throw the book against the wall. That's especially dangerous if they're reading an ebook. Do include senses other than sight. The dank, earthy scent of mushrooms growing on the tree. The stench of the factory smoke next door. The sound of cars whooshing by on the wet pavement.

In addition, consider when to start the scene. Do you have a lot of small actions that don't add to the final story? Consider chopping off the first half, and starting the scene in media res or in the middle of the action.

Next, move in closer. Who is in the scene? Is there more than one person? Are they interacting? Is it dialogue or action? Is there friendliness or tension? Does that change during this scene? A strong scene often has rising tension.

Does the scene forward the character arc? The plotline? Does it introduce a subplot, or complicate one? Introduce a new side character?

Most important, what does the character want in this scene? Every scene should have a goal, even if it's only a cup of water. That desire drives the purpose of the scene. Does your character solve a problem, or create a new one? Or are they recovering from the battle in the last scene? What else must be accomplished in this scene?

The last part of the scene should end on a high moment, something that makes the reader want to continue to the next chapter. Does your character get their goal? Or make it harder to achieve it? Are they foiled by an antagonist or their own poor decisions? How do they need to proceed in the next scene?

While it seems like a cheap ploy, cliffhangers are excellent at this. In my current WIP, I have a pilot about to land by moonlight on an unfamiliar airstrip. I cut the scene just before the plane hits the ground.

If your scene seems limp and useless, check it for the above points. It may be missing an essential item. Tweaking or rewriting the scene to include might save it from drowning in mediocrity!

CHAPTER ELEVEN: CHARACTERS GONE AWRY

So, what happens when you're a third through the first draft, and your characters refuse to cooperate? Never fear. This happens. Really, even for Extreme Planners, characters often get a life of their own and simply don't act the way you intended them to. This is a sign that you've crafted a good, well-rounded character, so there's that good news.

If this happens to your main character, you may wish to re-examine how you've crafted them, such as their goals and motivations. Perhaps you've designed them based on someone you know in real life or a character from a movie or book, and they're staying too close to their inspiration. Perhaps their motivation doesn't quite meld with the goal for the story. Or perhaps they're just being contrary to mess with your own sanity.

You have several options. You can modify the character, and hope they comply with their new parameters (unlikely). You can modify the plot so their motivations match the goal of the story. You can add a subplot or side character to change the dynamic and hope the character's personality will now comply with your plan. Sometimes you can do a combination of all these things.

Some people write a very clean first draft, and only modify what they have on their edits. Some cut entire scenes. Some move scenes around like index cards on a table (editing tools like Scrivener is helpful with this). Some do an entire rewrite on the second draft. Everyone edits with a different technique, and you may end up cutting huge swaths of your story.

I was about halfway through writing Past Storm and Fire, a dual-timeline time travel book set in modern Miami and medieval Iceland, when a new character showed up. She was the mother to the primary antagonist, and a witch. I had no idea she was going to be there, lurking in the forest when my main character escaped the antagonist's unwanted sexual advances. Her hut just sort of appeared as I wrote the scene, and she wouldn't go away.

I let it ride, to see how the character would interact with the story. She was too strong to be just a walk-on personality. She helped guide and mentor the main character, as an ersatz mother-figure. She literally gives everything to save the main character, and I cried when she died. It was a fitting ending for a wonderful character, but I'd never planned on her being there in the first place.

I didn't have to change the ending, but I did tweak the subplots and personal dynamics of the family to give her some more time interacting with the story. She helped add both color and mystery to the tale, and she had a memory twist that might become a prequel later on. That wasn't something I did on purpose, either! It just happened.

Another book with a surprise character was Call of the Morrigú, a paranormal adventure set in late 18th century Ireland. I'd done lots of research on historical characters during the Irish Rebellion of 1798, hoping to find one to include in my story. However, none of the personalities on record spoke to me, so I created one, a hedgewitch who believed in the Morrigan, and that belief lent the goddess earthly power. Her name was Old Nan. (I have a fascination with the old wise woman trope). I wove in her interactions as teacher and helper to both my main character and the goddess she roused. She also got to slap around some uppity young men, which was eminently satisfying.

If your character is going off-plan, it might be a flaw in your plan, and you can adjust as necessary. One reason why I use an Excel worksheet to hold my scene list is that it's very easy to cut/paste scenes in different places if I need to move things around, such as when adding a subplot or side character on the fly. It also allows me to see where I can add those subplot details in a roughly even manner through the rest of the book.

CHAPTER TWELVE:
THE AGONY AND THE ECSTASY

Now I'm into the "meat" of a novel, the daily slog and joy of writing each scene out. The boring part. "Sometimes it feels like shoveling shit from a sitting position" as per Stephen King. And sometimes, the most exciting part. You've got a placeholder first scene, maybe even a couple more. But you have a whole book to write! That's fine. That's what we signed up for. We can do this.

I love writing my scenes in the order that they will be in the book. Not everyone writes like that. And even as an extreme planner, you don't have to, either. You can write them as they occur to you. That's the beauty of a scene list! You know you'll eventually get to those scenes. So, if you dream of a perfect blocking for a fight scene, you can write that now and insert it as you write the others around it.

Sure, you can do this as a pantser, but you have much less chance of scrapping that scene because your pantsing went off in another direction. That gives a great chance at more creativity, but it's not so good at keeping your story on track.

DISCIPLINE

The first thing to keep in mind is that this is not a sprint. It's a marathon. Sprinters tend to get burned out quickly and quit. You don't churn out a 100,000-word novel in a weekend. It takes time, even for the most voracious planner.

I set myself a schedule that works for my lifestyle. I work full time, but I don't have children, so I have the luxury of being able to carve out my time as I wish. If you are a parent, especially of small children, this can be especially challenging. One author I know woke up at 4:30 am every day, an hour before her youngest children rose, to have time to dedicate to her writing. You do what you must.

I typically wrote during my lunch hour at work. Because I had already planned things out, I didn't need to waste that precious, limited time figuring out where I needed to go with the scene. I had been considering that over the last twenty-three hours, since I stopped writing the day before. I had a vision of what I wanted to happen and where it should end up.

I don't write one scene a day, in general. I go by word count, because I am numeric and goal-oriented. I set myself a 2,000 word a day minimum, with weekends off. That gives me, on average, 10,000 words a week, and 40,000 words a month. Which means, once my plan is done, I can write the first draft of a novel in about 2 months, give or take.

If I miss that, not too bad – I can usually make it up the next day or so. If I have too many misses, though, I have to give myself a stern talking to. Or at least admit that life has gotten the better of me and adjust my expectations. For one novel, it fought me the whole way, and I was happy to get 1,000 words a day for a full month. External stresses made it necessary, because life happens sometimes.

This is not for everyone, but it works for me. If I am on a roll, I can get those 2,000 words out in an hour, because I've already "pre-written" that scene in my head. By the time I get to my keyboard, I'm simply transcribing what I have already created into a document. It does help that I have a decent typing speed around 70 words per minute. It also helps that my writing style is very cinematic (according to feedback from others) and therefore I play the movie in my mind, and just write the script as it unfolds.

I do tend to give the setting a short shrift during my initial draft, so my second draft often involves fleshing out the physical details to get a better grounding.

> The purpose of a first draft is to exist.

Something else I do, as a goal-oriented person, is keep track of my progress. If I have 65 scenes planned out, and I've done 16 of them, that means my ending wordcount looks like it will be about 95K words. As I said earlier, my average scene length is 1,000-1,100 words. I have a calculation where I enter my total word count in my spreadsheet. It breaks out my daily word count, weekly word count, and keeps me going strong.

If I'm worried about things getting too short for a novel, I'll add a subplot or flesh out some scenes more deeply. If I'm worried about it being too long, I might remove one. However, I usually do neither until the second draft.

INCIDENTAL RESEARCH

Sometimes the subplots just pop up. In Misfortune of Vision, the main character, a 65-year-old grandmother, might have a friend. An old soldier, chief raider, cousin to her chief. Of course, she's cousin to the chief as well. Most of the older folk of the clan are related in some way to the chief. It's called a derbfine, anyone who shares a grandfather. It's from the derbfine that the next leader is usually chosen, not necessarily the son of the present one. That means a chief has to groom his chosen successor, and still it won't be assured. Men of the clan must choose the wisest leader.

Oh, I'm digressing down the path of historical research. Sorry! I do that a lot while writing. I get caught into a rabbit hole. Hopefully that research pays off later, but often it's just background information I keep in mind while writing.

What types of flowers would be growing on that hillside in 12th century Ireland in May? Did Vikings have a village nearby? What sort of foods would be sold at the market?

It is certainly possible to get so lost in the incidental research that you forget to write. Don't let it happen too often, or you'll never finish!

One of my author friends types [ELEPHANT] wherever she needs to come back to do incidental research, so her writing flow isn't interrupted. Such an insertion is easily found with scan/search functions later, during the editing phase.

CHARACTERS COMING TO LIFE

Now that I'm into the "meat" of my novel, my characters are beginning to come to life. Sometimes they come to life in ways I wasn't counting on. For instance, my main character, Orlagh, is becoming even more bitter and sarcastic than I had first imagined. And Clodagh has some sort of PTSD from childhood trauma. She also has manifested her gift of the Sight earlier than I had anticipated.

My antagonist, Declan, has turned into a sympathetic main character in his own right, with his own antagonist. The smith, Trygve, is becoming a great character. First a mentor, teaching Declan some basics of the blacksmithing art, then he becomes the Bad Guy by trying to take Declan's girl. It's all becoming much more complex than I had originally planned.

This is a good thing!

Even the best planner cannot plan everything in their novel.

I find it much easier to let the characters speak to me. At one point, I was going to have Declan pull a Jean Valjean, and steal from a priest who was kind to him. He told me in no uncertain terms that he was not that desperate, thank you very much. The priest was kind and he was honorable… at least for now.

Yes, this may mean adding scenes, deleting them, adding characters, changing subplots, and maybe even changing part of your main plot. Go with it. Your muse speaks through you and your characters. Go with the flow! Any other clichés I can throw out here? Oh, I know… Let it go!

CHAPTER THIRTEEN: THE DREADED WRITERS' BLOCK

WHAT IS IT?

Wikipedia defines Writer's Block as a condition, primarily associated with writing, in which an author loses the ability to produce new work or experiences a creative slowdown. Some authors experience it a lot, some not at all, some only during certain conditions. Many famous authors have suffered from it, including F. Scott Fitzgerald, Charles M. Schulz (Peanuts), Elizabeth Gilbert, and Herman Melville.

WHY DO WE GET IT?
- Distractions
- Illness
- Depression
- Personal issues with external life
- Running out of ideas
- Running out of inspiration
- Stuck on a plot point
- A scene isn't working but we don't know why

HOW TO COMBAT IT

- Take a self-care day – pamper yourself. Have a cup of hot chocolate. Take a nap. Watch an episode or two of your favorite brainless sitcom.
- Write about something else – anything else. Poetry. Word association. Write a word at the top of the page and just brainstorm about words associated with it. Don't worry about punctuation, grammar, or editing.
- Switch out to writing things out long hand – this engages a different thought process and can help mix things up a bit.
- Write a VERY short synopsis of where you are up to this point and finish the tale in your head – like three or four sentences, maximum.
- Break the routine – write somewhere else. Go to the coffee shop, the library, a hillside
- Treat writing like a job – set a time for it every day.
- Talk to friends about your writing problems – sometimes they can help you see what you're missing. They work as a sounding board.
- Study an aspect of writing – plot structure, character development, theme or subplot techniques
- Shut down the distractions – Shut down the social media, turn off your phone, close the door
- Take a cold shower – can reset your brain.
- Read your story aloud – Audial processing is different from visual processing.

- Stop trying to do it all at once – tackle one part of a scene at a time. Just write the scene, or just write the dialogue, or the action.
- Do some cleaning, go for a walk – but don't let this become a procrastination technique. It's too easy!
- Break the problem down into bits – Is the block because you don't know what comes next? Or because the character doesn't sound right? Or maybe you missed something in the past that you can't remember but needs to be addressed?
- Re-read your draft from the beginning – this can help you gel your ideas for the whole book and show where you need to go.
- Read good review of other books in your genre, to come up with inspiration on new things to do.
- Read bad reviews of other books in your genre, as ideas of what NOT to do.
- Write a letter to your character about why they aren't cooperating – "Why are you being so obstinate? I've given you everything, and you sit there, mute, with your mouth hanging open like a demented fish."
- Put on the soundtrack to a favorite or inspiring movie while you write – show tunes, classical music, whichever is your jam. If you like videogame soundtracks, they're specifically designed to help you focus on what is happening without distracting you.
- Play the scene in your mind like a movie – Imagine the blocking (where characters are standing/sitting), what they're wearing, what sort of lighting, etc.

- Read something – anything. Poetry, short stories, an excerpt from someone else's novel, your older work, etc.
- Peruse some visual art – use something particularly interesting as a writing prompt.
- Listen to your favorite songs for a day – nostalgia is a powerful tool to stir the imagination.
- Outline the scene – use phrases and words, rather than formal sentences. Start with the last scene if you need to.
- Skip the scene and move to the next one – write [FINISH SCENE HERE] or [TRANSITION HERE] and move on, if you know where you should be going and just can't figure out how to get there. Come back later when you've written more. The brackets make it easy to search them out.
- Exercise – anything that gets the blood pumping. Cleaning, cooking, crafting, gardening, something that keeps your hand busy and your mind free.
- Write the scene from the POV of a different character, even if you don't plan on having that POV in the final draft.
- Take a long drive, and imagine what life is like in the houses you pass, the people you see.
- Write down what you want that scene to accomplish.
- Write fast (no editing, no grammar) – no punctuation. No spelling. Just write. It helps to write "The worst draft" at the top to remind yourself it doesn't need to be good.
- Change your font to Comic Sans – seriously, some people say this helps them. It makes the font less intimidating and more playful.

- Find a critique group and join. The people in the group can be a fantastic resource, sounding board, or encouragement.

> Give yourself permission to write badly –
> This permission is important.
> It allows you to just get a draft down, as you can always edit later. You can't edit a blank page.

CHRISTY NICHOLAS

CHAPTER FOURTEEN: PROCRASTINATION AND THE FINISHED FIRST DRAFT

Procrastination is such a wonderful thing. How else would authors' houses ever get cleaned?

Many times, I've been facing a project that seemed too big, too difficult, too annoying, too boring, and ended up with a clean house, mowed yard, or even an organized craft room, something rarer than unicorns!

However, even as a lifelong procrastinator, I've managed to get a few things done over the years. It's so easy to fall into the trap, but it can also be escaped if you have the proper tools.

I'd like to note that many people have neurodivergence that prevents them from battling it the way neurotypical people do. If you have issues with executive disfunction, it might be wise to consult a mental health expert.

My favorite one is to start with little bites. The smallest part of your project, the easiest bit, the least annoying chunk. Or, at least the part you know how to do. Whittle away at the project until it looks less intimidating. Perhaps you're supposed to write a scene you aren't ready for – write the next one instead or skip several ahead.

Once you've completed some of the little bits, the rest might not look so intimidating.

Another tool I use is the opposite — tackle the biggest, worst, heaviest task first. Once you get this monster out of the way, the rest looks like easy-peasy work you can do in your sleep.

NaNoWriMo is another tool to battle the ever-present writers' procrastination disease. For those who haven't heard of it, it's National Novel Writing Month, held each November. Writers sign up and promise to write (not edit, just write!) 50,000 words during the month of November. There are support groups online and in real life, and you update your word count each day to keep track of your progress. You get badges and prizes when you complete goals, which is very helpful for goal-oriented folks. When you're done, you have a novel written! Or at least most of one.

Right now, I'm procrastinating on my WIP. To be fair, I do have some good excuses, and some not so good. Life got hectic for a while. Work got hectic as well, and I worked long hours at the end of the quarter. Then my editor sent me a set of edits on my last novel, which was due out in two months, and I had to work on that.

However, last night I submitted my first scene of my current WIP to my author group for critique. They loved it, but made some excellent suggestions about it, including a whole new opening scene. So, I may work on that before I add words. It will have to supplant this scene completely.

I also dreamt last night about a collection of five related short stories that I want to write about cats battling children's nightmares. But that must be tabled. I've written the idea down, so I can get to it later.

So many plot-bunnies!

There sometimes comes a point in your draft that you have many more interesting things to do. This seems to come to me about 2/3 through a draft. It just happened this point came at a time when I had three other novels in various stages of editing, and they all needed immediate attention.

Editing is a necessary evil, but it can also be a superb excuse for procrastination. Sometimes too superb.

As I've mentioned a few times, I'm goal-oriented. I also have what I call Project Completion Compulsion. That means I don't like starting a project until the current one is finished, at least through a defined stage. The first draft is such a stage. However, with those other editing projects, some of those were time-sensitive, as I had upcoming publication dates to be aware of.

This is when I found myself making more excuses. I found other projects more important, such as a promised review of someone's book or a promised beta read. However, that just meant I had been out of the project so long, I feared jumping in again. However, my need to finish projects is stronger than my need to procrastinate, in the end.

Several months later, after my pile of editing had been finished, I was finally free to start work again on Misfortune of Vision. After four months' hiatus, I wanted to do a full read-through edit of what I had so far.

While this took extra time, it had several benefits. First, I refamiliarized myself with the story details. Second, it meant I had most of the story already going through a first full edit (second draft). Third, it was a great exercise in getting back into the swing of things.

It took me about two weeks plus a few days to finish the first draft off at this point. I combined several planned scenes, but others took on a life of their own.

Near the end of the book, I get what I call "Light at the end of the Tunnel Speed," which means I get in far more than my normal 2,000 a day. I often get 5,000 words a day or more as I reach the finale, as I'm excited to be writing the climax, excited to be getting near the end of the draft, and just excited in general. My best day was a 13,700-word day. Which is a good chunk of the draft, if you think about it! A good 15% of an 80,000-word manuscript.

I'm a numbers girl, if you haven't realized that already. Therefore, here are some stats I came up with on this novel.

In total, the number of hours I estimate I spent on this first draft (just the writing, not the editing portion or the planning) was sixty hours for an 80,000-word first draft.

The research came to about thirty hours in addition to that. So far, editing had been only about six hours, but that total will go up dramatically in future weeks.

Every single author will have different stats. This is not a contest or comparison, but an example of how one author works. Someone else might take 500 hours to write their first draft, over the course of ten years. That's perfectly fine! You need to work in the manner that feels best to you.

It is an amazing feeling to finish the first draft of a novel. It's time to celebrate, no doubt! It's a fantastic hurdle, one that many people never achieve.

For the first novel, it was an adrenaline rush like being on a roller coaster. It's still a rush, but tempered by the knowledge of the amount of time, effort, pain and sweat is still to come in the editing process. After the first novel, you have no idea what's coming next. Now on my seventh novel, I am well aware I'm only about halfway done with this being in submittable form.

Keep in mind, I'm a fast writer. Do not ever compare your own speed to someone else's. We all write at our own paces. There are fast writers and slow writers, and any of them can be great writers.

PART THREE: EVIL EDITING
CHAPTER FIFTEEN: EDITING TYPES

So, you've finished your first draft. Congratulations! That's an incredible hurdle! So many would-be authors never finish their first draft of their first novel. It deserves celebration, kudos, and a nice big drink of the alcoholic persuasion.

Now reality kicks in. In fact, it might kick in so hard, it breaks the door.

Now, some people enjoy editing. I don't understand these people in the slightest, but everyone is different. Those who love it sometimes end up doing it for a living. I am not those people.

Editing is, for me, the most painful process of writing, even harder than getting out that first draft. However, there are several different types of editing, and several different stages you can go through with your edits.

I'll say this now, and likely repeat it later. Pay for professional editing. No matter how good you think you are at grammar, story construction, or proofreading, a professional editor is what takes your work from amateur to professional. It is absolutely worth the price. Don't skimp here! All the Extreme Planning in the world is not enough to ignore this step. Even if you are an editor yourself.

Below is a brief overview of each stage of the editing process I go through. Afterward, I'll delve more deeply into some of them.

CRITIQUE PARTNERS

A critique partner is usually another author, possibly a personal friend, who writes within your genre. This partner will work with you as you hammer out your synopsis, and work as a sounding board as you throw out ideas. Often, you are doing the same for them as they work out a draft. It's someone you can message as an idea pops up, and run it by them as a feasible addition to your story. They can ask questions, poke holes in the idea, offer more suggestions to refine it, and so on. It's an organic process, and very useful, but not something everyone wants, likes, or has access to.

ALPHA READER

An alpha reader is usually someone who reads your work as it comes out, perhaps chapter by chapter. Again, this is someone who is a friend or fellow author, and again, it's not something every author wants, likes, or has access to. However, alphas can offer great advice on plots that need more attention, or subplots that just aren't working, characters they like and think should have a greater role in the story, etc.

FIRST ROUND EDITS

This part might just take longer than writing the first draft. This is addressed in **Chapter Fifteen**.

OPENING SCENE AND FIRST LINES

At this point, I usually go back and rewrite the opening scene of my novel. This is explained in greater detail in **Chapter Seven**.

SECOND DRAFT EDITS

Oh, look! Another separate Chapter! Are you annoyed yet? Good. You're prepped for the annoyance of editing. More information will come in **Chapter Seventeen**.

BETA READING

Yet another separate chapter! I cover this extensively in **Chapter Eighteen**.

LINE-BY-LINE GRAMMAR EDITING

I put this next because I prefer to give my professional editor as clean of a manuscript as I can. That cuts down on their time and allows them to concentrate less on the grammar and spelling and more on the developmental and construction issues.

To do this, I use a tool. There are several out there, such as Grammarly and Scrivener, but I prefer ProWritingAid. There are free versions and there are paid versions. For me, it's well worth the $100 I paid for lifetime access. I have used all three and much prefer the breadth of options ProWritingAid offers.

Editing software helps me go through each chapter and highlights the areas where my grammar seems off, or my pacing is slow, or I've mixed U.K. spellings of words with U.S. spellings (colour vs. color).

Editing software also highlights overused words for me. It points them out in judgmental highlights and offers suggestions on how many I should remove to be in line with other writing. It finds clichés, both in and out of dialogue. Of course, it highlights misspelled words and grammar errors, but there are so many other tools, it's well worth it.

PROFESSIONAL EDITING

As I mentioned earlier, even the best Extreme Planner, no matter how clean you think your manuscript is, will need professional editing. That's not just one editor, either. There are several different levels of editing. While a good alpha and/or beta reader might help, and editing software is a boon, it's a great idea to get your manuscript as clean as possible before paying for an editor.

Editing types:
- Developmental and Structural Editing
    - Story arc
    - Scene progression and structure
    - Contents gaps
    - Character development
    - Logical consistency and coherence
    - Pacing
    - Fact and anachronism checking
    - Balance between dialogue, action, and exposition

- Line and Copy Editing
    - Style (tense, show vs. tell, etc.)
    - Sentence structure
    - Paragraph structure
    - Dialogue
    - Word usage--repeated/overused words
    - Passive voice
    - Tone
    - Filter words (heard, saw, felt, etc.)

- Proofreading/Mechanical editing
    - Missing words
    - Homonyms (affect/effect, to/two/too)
    - Spelling
    - Grammar
    - Punctuation and abbreviations

- Formatting
- Capitalization

ADDRESSING SUGGESTED EDITS

My professional editor sends me a Word document with my manuscript. It contains two types of edits. The easier type is adding or subtracting commas, correcting words (waterskin to water skin, towards to toward, etc.) and the like. I just look at each one and decide (usually) to accept the correction. Occasionally I will decline it because it is part of someone's authentic speech pattern, or an archaic spelling that works better with the story. I'll leave a comment bubble for her explaining the rejection.

The second type of edits are comment bubbles. Those often take longer to correct. Some are easy, such as "this is an awkward sentence" or "your timeline is off here, please fix." Other times it's more difficult, such as "Your pacing is off here. You might want to pick it up last scene," or "Your main character has a similar internal conflict to the last book in this series. You may want to choose something different."

Once I address comments, I also have my own to correct. You see, the three months between me submitting the manuscript to the publisher and my editor returning it for edits were not spent idle. Not only did I write another novel in the meantime, I thought about this one. I cogitated. I percolated. I came up with interesting tidbits that could improve the story, the character, the setting. I made notes of these epiphanies in my copy of the document so I could make those changes when their edits came around.

Since I'd already written most of the next book, I used that time to tie in some of the events of the other novel, to more easily mesh the overarching story. Details of characters that are in both, that sort of thing.

Now that the editor has the manuscript once again, she'll go through for a second and usually third level of edits, sending each to me in turn to correct. So now we wait, again.

> Beta readers and good editors are gold.
> Annoying them or taking umbrage at their suggestions only serves to shoot yourself in your foot.

If you don't agree with their suggestions, you have several options. First, you may nod, smile, and do your own thing. Second, you might ask why they make that suggestion, as it may be a good reason, or you may explain it later in your narrative. Third, you can get defensive and ensure they won't help in the future. Your call.

PROOFREADING

This is the final step before getting a manuscript ready for publication, and it's the most nitpicky portion. This is usually better

done by a professional editor, as proofreading is consistent with the latest version of The Chicago Manual of Style.
- Proofreading
  - Typos
  - Grammar
  - Spelling
  - Capitalization
  - Punctuation
  - Formatting
    - Paragraph consistency (indentation, scene breaks, etc.)
    - Number, time (year, clock) consistency (e.g., 10 vs ten)

Sometimes, when you are working on multiple books, it can get difficult to remember where you are with any one manuscript, and what you still have to do on each. I keep a spreadsheet (of course, I do!) of where I am on each book, including who has volunteered to be a beta reader.

	Synopsis	Scene list	Characters Profiles	First Draft	First Edit	Second Edits	Line by Line Edit	First Betas	Second Betas	Pro Editor
Better To Have Loved	X	X	X	X	X	X	X	X	X	X
Legacy of Hunger	X	X	X	X	X	X	X	X	X	X
Legacy of Truth	X	X	X	X	X	X	X	X	X	X
Taming of the Few	X	X	X	X	X	X	X	X	X	
Much Ado About Dying	X	X	X	X						
Extreme Planning	X	X	X	X	X	X	X	X	X	X

		Book Cover Art			Formatting				Pre-order Setup				
					Amazon		Ingram Spark		Draft 2 Digital	Smash words	Amazon		Ingram Spark
	Blurb	eBook	Print	Audio	eBook	Print	eBook	Print	eBook	eBook	eBook	Print	Print
Better To Have Loved	X	X	X	X	X	X	X	X	X	X	X	X	X
Legacy of Hunger	X	X	X	X	X	X	X	X	X	X	X	X	X
Legacy of Truth	X	X	X	X	X	X							
Taming of the Few													
Much Ado About Dying													
Extreme Planning		X											

ORGANIZATION EXERCISE: Set up a spreadsheet with the various steps toward the published project.

CHAPTER SIXTEEN:
FIRST ROUND OF EDITS AND ALL THE PAIN

Once your first draft is finished, you have a choice. You can either take a break, work on something else for a while to clear your palate, or dive right into the first round of edits.

I recommend taking a break for a few reasons. First, it allows you to gain some distance from your project, and lets you forget details.

> If we are too familiar with the story,
> our mind fills in details it knows rather than reading
> what's actually on the page.

That's how we miss errors when we're doing a read-through of our own work. Our brain knows what it's supposed to say, and sometimes skims the details, trusting them to be correct. It's also how we miss obvious clues about the setting or the character that are in our minds, but never made it into the story. This is where beta readers will come in, but that comes later.

This first round is when you, the author, take a fresh look at your manuscript from the beginning. Even as an Extreme Planner, the shape and flavor of the novel will have changed from when you first started. There may be hints you left in chapter one that you forgot to address later, or a subplot you added that needed a breadcrumb earlier on. Your main character may have morphed into a different personality than you originally planned. This readthrough allows you to fix those continuity errors and tighten the consistency in plot, character, setting, and structure.

While I percolated after the first draft, I'd emailed myself notes to fix the storyline as they occurred to me. This is more planning, "pre-writing", making the most of the time you can't physically write to prepare for your limited keyboard time.

This is also a time the plots refine in my mind. As I lay falling asleep, I decide I need another appearance from the Bishop near the end, and I need to make certain another character forgets an important detail. Or I need to add a character. Perhaps I want to increase the tension in another scene. More description in that scene, less in the other.

Add a character here. Increase the stakes there. No, that character should react more like this. And I have to do a complete read-through (yes, despite doing one on the first portion recently after I took my break) to make certain all the details, timeline, subplots mesh and agree. In my last novel, The Enchanted Swans, I had a shift in the children's ages, and got confused as to who was how old and when. But that novel took place over the course of 900 years. Since this new novel only takes place in a couple months' time, age isn't a factor, but the dates are. My climax scene is based on an historical battle that has a mostly precise date (late February) so I needed to make certain my timeline matched. Most of the characters are older. Passing time takes on less significance for adult characters than for children, at least in terms of their changing reactions to events.

With a deep sigh, I open the manuscript, address any notes I've made above with spot changes, and dive into my least favorite part of the whole process. Wish me luck!

I also find myself nixing my favorite words, such as "just," "simply," "finally," "could," "perhaps/maybe," and the dreaded "was" and "were," which often indicates passive voice. I try to minimize the word "said," without using too many intrusive substitutes, such as "he responded" or "she growled." Instead, I shift to action tags where I can.

While there is nothing inherently wrong with any of these words, I know that I personally overuse them, and often the work is stronger if I remove them or at least change them up to offer the reader some variety.

"Was" and "were" are different matters. Yes, they are required words. However, they often herald passive sentence structure. Active structure is more dynamic to a reader and allows for more immediate action. So, I minimize the use of these words during that read-through. This is not something you must do in this editing stage, but it should be something you take a look at at some point.

CHAPTER SEVENTEEN: DRAFT NUMBER TWO, ELECTRIC BUGALOO

Writing my first draft takes about two months, as long as life doesn't interfere horribly. That's a long time to keep the details of your story in mind, especially in the throes of creation. Once you're done, though, it's time to tackle the hard part.

You've played with your opening scene so it's time for draft two. I find this the most difficult slog of all, the one that I'm most likely to procrastinate. Why is that? Because I'm not creating things anew, but editing what I've already done. I'm familiar with it, so it's less exciting to read. I skip over parts because I know it, but that's exactly what you aren't supposed to do at this point.

A fellow author friend of mine calls her second draft a rewrite, and she literally rewrites the entire draft. However, she's a discovery writer, and this may really be her first draft, with her nominal first draft being more equivalent to my synopsis (albeit longer and more detailed). Regardless, the process works for her.

Remember,

> Every single author works in a different way,
> due to different strengths,
> passions, talents, and motivations.
>
> Finding your own best way is the only thing you need to do. This book, as well as any other writing book, can only help you find that best way for yourself.

Now, a great trick to help me get over the "boringness" of editing the second draft is to **put the project aside** for a while and work on something else. This works to cleanse my palette, create some distance between me and this project. Since I typically layer my novels, this often works out well. After the first draft of Legacy of Luck, book three, is done, I can work on the editing for Legacy of Truth, book two. Then I'll work on the final edits of Legacy of Hunger, book one. Or I can work on the planning stages of Misfortune of Vision, book four. Even if you don't have another project to work on, take a break. A couple weeks, if you can.

Once you've given yourself that space, you can start re-reading the novel from the beginning, with a critical eye. The things I look for in a second draft, and correct as I read:

- Tie up subplots and story threads I started early in the book and forgot to address later. This happens to me a lot, as I leave

breadcrumbs early on, thinking I'm so clever, and completely forget they exist halfway through the first draft.
- Character arcs that don't make sense. Wait, they started out as a whiner, why are they now this grand adventurer? Split them into two people, or give them some reason for the change.
- Flesh out under-described scenes (or cut down over-described scenes). I tend to bull through scene descriptions in my first draft, since I write so fast. I love the descriptions, so I know I'll come back and work on them later.
- Vary the actions of characters (I tend to have lots of them cross their arms, clench their fists, or nod. So many nodding characters. It's like a bobble-doll festival in my first drafts.)
- Fix unbelievable/wooden dialogue. My first drafts usually have flat dialogue, or characters with very similar voices. This is where I can vary it to make my characters unique and identifiable. Brandon Sanderson says that if he can figure out what character is speaking without a dialogue tag, you've done a good job.
- Flesh out high-action scenes, especially around the climax of the novel. Because it's high action, I tend to write these scenes quickly, as it's playing in my head and I only type so fast. Going back to fill in the details I see but didn't write helps a lot.
- Fill in plot holes. There are always plot holes. So many plot holes.
- If I've changed character names, or added/removed one, ensure they're all changed. My latest urban fantasy novel started off with a family of twelve hosting the main characters. I realized I had to simmer that down to a family of six, and it was still a lot.

- Punch up the tension in every scene. I always need more tension, as I tend to write drawing room-level boring in my first draft.
- Cut out excess scenes that don't add to the plot or character arc. This can be difficult, and where the phrase "kill your darlings" applies. Yes, I know you love that scene with the vicar serving tea, but what does it really accomplish? Can you add a sentence to the next scene referencing the action and accomplish the same effect? Do it.
- Fill in flat characters. Make sure each one has motivation, personality, and a purpose. Combine side characters if need be. Ensure each has at least a rudimentary description or prominent characteristic. Maybe cut a bunch of characters out.

Going through my entire draft a second time usually takes a much shorter time than the first draft. Instead of two months, it often takes about three weeks, if I'm not procrastinating. Which I do! However, I tend to procrastinate by working on other writing projects, so that's fine. However, eventually you need to get back to this one.

Despite all the pain, it's invaluable to read your draft several times to refine and polish the storyline, characters, setting, action, dialogue, etc. Some authors prefer to do themed passes, i.e., read once just for character, read once just for dialogue, which allows them to remain in a focused mindset through the entire book. Others prefer to read it as a reader would, letting the story coalesce in their mind as it progresses. Reading it aloud or having a tool like Whispersync read it can be another tool.

> No matter how diligently you read your draft, though, even if you're on the tenth run through, there comes a time when you, as the author, become blind to the words on the page. You know what you meant to write, and your mind sees your intent, rather than the words you've actually written. That's when you need outside help.

Yes, you need outside help. No, you shouldn't do this all alone. Beta readers, editors, proofreaders – none of these are tasks that the author should do.

Now, if you happen to have extensive training as an editor… nope, you still shouldn't be relying upon only yourself to edit your work. You're too close to it. You will miss the forest for the trees. Fresh eyes are the best when it comes to editing.

That will bring us to our next chapter.

CHAPTER EIGHTEEN: BETA READERS OR HOW TO ALIENATE YOUR FRIENDS AND FAMILY

Beta readers are more precious than gold. They are the wonderful folks who read your manuscript with fresh eyes. This is after you've done edits. They can do developmental editing, concentrating on story structure, character arcs, story pacing, etc. that you've become blind to after writing the bloody thing and reading through it three or four times already.

Fresh eyes are absolutely necessary at this point to find the glaring errors, and even some of the subtle ones. Usually beta readers are other authors, you might be beta reading their own draft in exchange. Sometimes they are better at the big picture, or perhaps at line-by-line grammar edits. Each one has its strengths. Each one is invaluable.

A note: When these lovely folks give you feedback, don't get defensive. Don't get angry. Don't say, "it's just a draft." You aren't defending a thesis for your doctorate. You're asking a boon from someone to spend a great deal of time and effort with the aim to improving your work. If you offend them, they won't help again. And you will have lost a valuable resource, and possibly a friend.

Please do not send your first draft to beta readers. A beta reader is someone who helps you with editing as a second set of eyes, but is not a formal editor and (usually) not paid for their feedback. They are often friends, family, fellow authors, or readers interested in the genre.

The first draft is rough. If you send it off to these precious beta readers, they will concentrate on the big changes you could have fixed yourself. Then they are "used up" and already know the story. Therefore, they're no longer a great resource for the next draft, where you need fresh eyes. Save them for a tighter draft.

The story, at this point, is living in your mind. Your imagination has all the motives, back story, and characteristics firmly entrenched for each character. However, if you haven't given hints of these in the manuscript itself, the readers won't understand them. A good beta reader will help point out this lack.

They ask questions like, "Why did Esme choose Sean? Alan was much nicer to her," or "this paragraph is awkward," or "wait, didn't that guy get killed off in chapter three?"

The beta reader can tell you when a scene falls flat or doesn't seem relevant. They can warn you that a character arc doesn't seem sufficiently strong, or they have no agency. They are valuable feedback on your story as you refine it.

Always thank your beta readers, both in person and in your acknowledgements, if you can. If a beta reader gives you feedback you absolutely disagree with, maybe ask for more clarification. Perhaps they worded their critique poorly. If you still disagree, move on. It is up to you whether to act on their advice, but they've taken precious time to read your book and offer advice. Thank them even if you disagree with that feedback. Regardless, they've put in a great deal of time and effort to help you make your book better. It's a lot of work. Even if you disagree with what they say, thank them for their time and smile. Betas are gold. They are diamonds. They are... my preciousssss.

The hardest part of using beta readers is waiting. What if they hate it? What if it's a total mess? And since beta reading is such a labor-intensive task, it takes a while. A month, maybe more. I'm currently beta reading a book for another author and have spent about 20 hours on it so far.

Some authors exchange chapters at a time, but I prefer the whole manuscript. I lose track if I'm sending chapters, especially to more than one reader. Also, people read at different paces depending on their mood. They might go through three chapters in a sitting if they're in the zone.

Sometimes you send your book to a beta reader and they never get back to you. This may be for a variety of reasons, but unless they outright tell you it's because they hate the book, don't assume that. Real life often gets in the way of a beta reader's promise, which is why I try to get my book out to at least six or seven readers, with the expectation that three or four will get feedback to me.

Once the beta readers return their comments to you, it's time for more edits. You may agree with those edits, or you may disagree. It's totally up to you, they just suggest.

> If several betas say the same thing, you may want to re-examine that bit carefully.

I have a diverse group of beta readers for my current novel in age, gender, experience, education, and outlook. That gives me a wide breadth of feedback.

The first one was an excellent critique. He pointed out some huge inconsistencies in one character's reactions. I fixed that by making her under the influence of a mad Fae lord. One thing fixed. Another was not enough sympathy for another character. I fixed that by inserting him earlier in the narrative, giving more time for the reader to interact with them. A third character was given more parts earlier on, as well, to make certain he became a larger part of the story. I tied in some loose ends. I fixed some grammar issues and anachronistic language.

> **BETA READER EXERCISE:** Make a list of friends and family who might make useful and willing beta readers. Make sure they are people who are willing to give you real feedback, not just pleasant platitudes. Those are lovely and ego-boosting but don't help you improve your craft.

Then find at least two beta readers who are not friends and family. An author critique group. Online (Absolute Write Water Cooler and Scribophile are excellent resources for advice and beta readers. There are also several Facebook groups dedicated to this).

I don't fool myself that all issues were addressed, but a good chunk of them have made the book better. After 2-3 more critiques, the book might be ready for another full read-through and edit.

After I receive my beta read drafts, I will edit and then edit some more. Perhaps send out the draft again after that, if I feel I need to get more feedback, or if I change a major portion of the story.

For those keeping track, my time so far on this novel:

About 25 hours research before I started
3 hours setting up the synopsis, characters, scene list
55 hours writing the first draft (over 4 months' time)
20 hours editing
Total so far: 102 hours, and I ain't done yet.

> It can be maddening and frustrating waiting for beta readers to finish their critique and get that feedback into your eagerly awaiting hands. In the meantime, direct that nervous energy into a new project.
> See, Extreme Planning!

My next project was the prequel to the first book. This was titled Misfortune of Song, and will involve the main character of this book, Orlagh. However, instead of being a 65-year-old sarcastic grandmother, she's now a 17-year-old foolish girl with lovesick eyes.

And sarcasm. And the main character is her grandfather Maelan, a stiff-necked old soldier who just wants to protect his family.

Good luck with that, Maelan.

I've written up a two-page synopsis, a set of characters, and the scene list. I've done some research on place/location/historical characters and found a good place and a good conflict to work as a backdrop to this story.

Next is writing chapter one.

See how it layers in? The waiting period for book one is filled with starting book two. By the time I'm done with my first draft, I might have all my beta readers done. I can do that last edit and submit to my publisher just in time to do the first full edit of this one.

And so, the cycle goes.

PART FOUR: TRADITIONAL PUBLISHING PATH

CHAPTER NINETEEN: THE QUERYING PROCESS

I shall begin this section by reminding you that there is no one way to write a book. Likewise, there is no one way to send a query. As the saying goes, there is more than one way to skin the cat, but none are pleasant for the cat. This is merely how I've learned to do things, and hopefully this will work for you as well. It is outside the scope of this book to explore all the techniques and formats used.

While there's a fairly standard format for query letters, understand that each literary agency (and sometimes each literary agent within an agency) will add their unique requirements in terms of the entire "query package."

Please, follow their instructions to the letter. An agent may view any deviation from instructions as a reason to put your work on the "slush pile" and move onto another author who followed directions. This is their first exposure to working with the author. If that author can't follow basic instructions, they may prove difficult to work with.

All that said, the query letter itself will follow a general format:

Your Name
Address
email
date

Agent's Address

Personalized greeting: Dear or Greetings (find the agent's name and spell it correctly!)

- Hook paragraph: The initial sentence about your book to grab the agent's attention.
- Summary paragraph: A summary about your book, the plot, character, etc.
- Bio paragraph: A bit about yourself and your experience as an author
- Closing: A thank you and a request for them to review your manuscript.

THE HOOK PARAGRAPH

The hook is your first (and sometimes, only) chance to grab the agent's attention. The first sentence should be strong. Make it punchy. Make it interesting. Make it unique. There are several formats commonly used. Sure, it's a formula, but it's a formula that works.

When X wants Y, Z happens. X wins by doing W.

"When [such-and-such event] happens, [main character] must [further conflict] and triumph in their own special way."

Example:
When the evil Empire destroys his family's farm, Luke must learn an ancient art and overcome the lies of his past.

Some other options for setting up your hook are below:

Give an interesting era/location
Set in modern-day Jerusalem…
During the summer of 1889 in a rural Texas town…
Taking place in turn-of-the-century New York City…

Describe a unique main character

The tale of Una Spencer, wife of Melville's legendary fictional whale harpooner Captain Ahab…

A chatty cozy mystery starring 50-something college professor Bell Barrett…

Narrated by Cot Daley, an Irish peasant girl kidnapped from Galway and sent to Barbados…

Examples of hook paragraphs (via AgentyQuery.com):

Bridges of Madison County

When Robert Kincaid drives through the heat and dust of an Iowa summer and turns into Francesca Johnson's farm lane looking for directions, the world-class photographer and the Iowa farm wife are joined in an experience that will haunt them forever.

The Kite Runner

An epic tale of fathers and sons, of friendship and betrayal, that takes us from Afghanistan in the final days of the monarchy to the atrocities of the present.

The Da Vinci Code

A murder in the silent after-hour halls of the Louvre Museum reveals a sinister plot to uncover a secret that has been protected by a clandestine society since the days of Christ.

All of this takes a lot of work, trial and error, and feedback from others. Many authors spend hours crafting a great hook. Then hours more to revise it. And you can craft multiple hooks to use in different queries (they can be used in advertising, too). However, there's a shortcut, thanks to being an Extreme Planner.

> **HOOK EXERCISE:** Remember that first sentence you wrote at the beginning of the book, the one with the main conflict and character? Go get that. Massage the words so they are emotionally charged, concise, and intriguing. Craft that into your hook paragraph.

The rest of the first paragraph should include, at the very least, the following things:

- **Title of your book:** Always include it. Some put it in all capitals, italics, or bold to make certain it stands out.
- **Genre:** So, you've written a historical romance time-travel women's fiction with some adventure and paranormal elements. Don't tell them all that. It's a quick way to make them toss the query. If you can't narrow down your genre to a few main ones, they can't market it. Choose one genre, and maybe add "with a thread of" another. Choose two at most. This is not the time to be cute, and you don't need to highlight every single aspect of your story. If you can't distill the genre, read some samples of them and narrow it down.
- **Word count:** Very important. Many agents won't touch novels below or above certain word counts. Also, this is a strong indicator that you have completed your manuscript, which is also important. Agents won't work with an unfinished story. This can be an estimate (90,000). Certain genres have certain standards. Romances and cozy mysteries tend to be lower, while epic fantasy tends to run higher, due to world-building.
- **Relationship?** Have you met the agent at a conference? Did they like your tweet on a pitch day? Do they have listed in their MSWL (Manuscript Wish List) that they love paranormal romance? If you have a special connection, mention it briefly. However, if you found them in a database, you don't need to mention that.

THE SUMMARY PARAGRAPH

The summary paragraph can be the most difficult part of a query. How to distill a 100K word epic into one paragraph, and still retain the magic? That's pretty much impossible, but you still have to get as close as you can. Read the backs of your favorite novels to get a feel for the format and tone of professional blurbs. Take your hook and expand it into a mini-plot.

> Be careful not to give away your ending. Literary Agents like to be surprised just like readers do.

Brainstorm. Write down words, spit them out, rearrange them, try a bunch of combinations. For my book, I might form a word cloud like this:

Adventure. Historical. Fairy. Vikings. Family. War. Battle. Age. Legacy. Descendant. Grandchild. Norman. Fort. Irish. Ireland. Celtic. Cold. Winter. Warrior. Prophecy. Seer. Cassandra.

Then craft those words into sentences. I would start with three sentences. First, describe the character (not necessarily name them). Then describe the dilemma they face. Third, explain what is at stake if they make the wrong choice or action.

Make certain the conflict is clear. Strong story is driven by conflict, and the biggest critique I see on any blurb or query is that the conflict is not described or unclear. The second biggest critique is that the stakes are missing or not high enough.

In addition to the above, convey what makes your story intriguing or unique. Does your story explore racism in ancient Rome? Does it address domestic violence on a future world? Does it describe a hero's journey in an unexpected place? Is it a feel-good romance set in modern-day China? Every story has something unusual to highlight.

Once you've distilled the information above, it's time to craft the summary paragraph. Once again, our path as an Extreme Planner already has a shortcut for that.

> **SUMMARY PARAGRAPH EXERCISE:** Go back to the first paragraph you created to plan your book. The one which described your main character, their primary goal, and what's stopping them from that goal. This is your essential story. Use this as the bones of your summary paragraph, and then 'beautify' the words to be as attractive, intriguing, and interesting as you can. Pump up the conflict and stakes.

THE BIO PARAGRAPH

Even if you've never published anything before nor won any awards, you can still have a strong bio section. Have you gotten a degree in History and you're writing historical fiction? Have you attended a Writers' Workshop? Are you a police officer, like your main character? Have you published a few stories in a literary magazine? However, keep it short and sweet and directly related to this book. The agent doesn't need your entire memoir.

BIO EXERCISE: Look up a one-paragraph biography of an author you like. Using that as a guide, write up three sentences about yourself. Where you live, what your hobbies are, what your writing credits are, if any. Be funny and quirky, if you like. While most parts of the query letter should be serious, making the agent smile here is fine.

THE CLOSING PARAGRAPH

Say thank you! Agents appreciate a thank you. Be polite. Say you're looking forward to hearing from them. Mention you appreciate their time and consideration. If you've ever written a cover letter for a resume in a job search, similar factors can apply here.

ATTACHMENTS

If the agent requests the first five or ten pages on their site, they usually ask that it be copied and pasted into the body of the email, rather than added as an attachment. Most agents will not open attachments, for fear of viruses.

If they request the first ten pages, and you panic because you don't know what font size or page size they want, relax. The standard measurement of a page is 250 words, so a ten-page sample would be about 2,500 words. This is just a guideline, so don't stop in the middle of a sentence. If it's reasonable within the guidelines, stop at the end of a scene or chapter.

Do stop at a cliffhanger, if possible.
This will help entice the agent to request more.
(insert Evil Laugh here)

DO'S OF YOUR QUERY LETTER

- **Research your options!** Some agents simply aren't the right fit for your book, your personality. There are lots of small and starting publishers out there that may not suit your goals. For example, many only do ebooks, or have less-than-stellar covers and/or editing. Others may do no marketing for their authors at all (most don't have big budgets unless you're a big name).
- **Read the Guidelines.** If the agent's site says to include the genre, include it. If they say to include the first five pages, don't include ten. If they ask about your social media presence, give a few examples. Each agent has different requirements.
- **Do address the query letter directly to an agent.** This proves you've done some homework.
- **Be professional.** Don't curse, don't use text-speak, don't "chat," don't use first person in the letter itself. **Note:** the story summary might use first person if the manuscript is in first person.
- **Keep it simple!** One page, 250-300 words, max. Single spaced, 12-point font. Left aligned. Don't get cute or creative here, trying to stand out by being different. There's a time and a place for that, and the query letter isn't it. You can have a clever bit in your bio, as I mentioned earlier.
- **Use short sentences and short paragraphs.** Agents get hundreds of letters each month and must skim through them all. Long sentences can be difficult to understand on a quick reading, and the agent loses interest.

- Try to **keep the tone of your query similar to the tone of your story** while keeping it professional. If you have a psychological thriller, the summary paragraph might be somber and dark, as opposed to a YA (Young Adult) slice-of-life book which would have a lighter, more jaunty tone.
- **Let someone else proofread it!** Just like a resume, typos are death knells.
- **IF the agent asks for comps** (comparative titles like your own), include a few. However, don't say, "This is the next Harry Potter!" This is hubris, over-selling, and a sign of an amateur.
- **Make every word count.** This is your entire novel, incredibly distilled. Have you ever had to reduce a lot of information into 280 characters for a tweet? Similar idea.
- **Some agents/publishers may be scams**, charging "reading fees," or geared toward selling marketing packages. Others ask for money up front for editing or cover art. If their website looks geared toward authors and not readers, then they are likely earning their money from authors, not readers. That means your books won't sell – but they'll be making money off you. This violates AAR ethics (Association of Authors Representatives). See link in resources for a place to check them out.
- **Pitch one book at a time.** If you plan to make the book into a series, you might mention that it has "series potential." On the other hand, if you have already written the series, definitely mention it, as that is a plus for any agent.
- **Leave the punctuation conservative!** No exclamation points!! Certainly not two or three!!!

- Some agencies with multiple agents say "A no from one of us is a no from all of us." Pay attention to this. Others say, "Another agent within the agency might be a better fit." In the latter case, feel free to query another, after the original agent rejects your manuscript. Some may even pass on the query to a different agent within the agency, if they think it's a good fit.

DON'TS OF THE QUERY LETTER

- **Don't write, "This work is copyrighted."** By U.S. law, your work is copyrighted the moment you write it. Saying your work is copyrighted wastes space and looks unprofessional. In addition, an agent may take offense to the implication that they'd steal your work.
- **Don't say this work is "partially auto-biographical."** Reason: all fictional works have some element of autobiography—you're wasting valuable query space here!
- **Don't over-sell with hyperbole or cliché.** "The best new novel of the decade!" "This story will knock your socks off!" "Enthralling, brilliant, one-of-a-kind!" This belongs on your cover when you get editorial reviews, not on your query. Don't tell the agents what they will think. This also holds true with saying it's "interesting" or "intriguing."
- **Don't apologize for being unpublished or a newbie.** Everyone was a newbie once. Everyone was unpublished once. Yes, even Stephen King. He received thirty rejections for Carrie before someone took a chance on it.

- **Don't try to convert the agent.** If an agent says in their online bio or manuscript wishlist that they're not interested in crime fiction, don't pitch them in the first place.

DON'TS IN THE QUERY PROCESS

- **Don't send a query to every literary agent you like at the same time.** What you learn in rejections from one agent might help you refine your query and hook for the next agent.
    - It is generally acceptable or recommended to send a maximum of 6-8 queries per week.
- **Don't follow up unless their website says it's allowed to follow up.** "No response means a rejection," is much more common than, "Feel free to contact us again if you don't hear from us in six weeks."
- **Don't reply to rejections, even to thank them.** Even if it seems polite, it just adds to the amount of correspondence an agent must dig through each day.
- **Don't insult other authors, books, or agents in your query or correspondence.** Agents talk to each other! Not long ago, a story about an author who was publicly rude to an agent went viral. Many other agents read it. Guess who never got a book deal?

ONLINE PITCHING CONTESTS

Above, when discussing the relationship the author might have with the agent, I mentioned pitching contests. For those unfamiliar with this trend, I'll delve into them more deeply here.

Most of these are through Twitter, and if you're unfamiliar with Twitter in general or pitching contests in particular, it would be a good idea to create an account (it's free!). If you like, you can make an anonymous account. You can follow authors or agents you like, and see what they're looking for or how they interact. If you don't like an agent's Twitter banter, they may not be a good fit for you or your work.

You can search back through hashtags (#PitchMadness, #PitMad,#PitRom, etc.) to see the kinds of pitches and tags used for past contests. Some contests maintain separate web pages with details about the contest (date/time of contest, what you might win, etc.). Sometimes they're purely about exposure to agents for small publishing presses, but sometimes they're geared toward finding a critique partner or a mentor.

- Create a pitch for your book.
- Twitter allows you 240 characters (including spaces and punctuation) so you must create a pitch that delivers character, conflict, and stakes in a concise manner.
- If you can't get your pitch to fit without devolving into semi-intelligible abbreviations and emojis, then some contest communities offer feedback sessions to improve your pitch.
- Getting an eye-catching comparison title (other work that your book resembles) can be an important way of getting an agent's

attention. Comps books, film, television, movies, or video games. You can include more than one if you have the space.
- o You also want a comp that is well known enough to be useful. Let's say you've written a book that is a retelling of Snow White, but it's set in the modern day and centers around thrilling political intrigue. A comp might be "SNOW WHITExTHE WEST WING".
- o Another comp format is "For fans of Outlander" or "For fans of Downton Abbey"
- You need to reserve some of those characters for "tagging" your Twitter post. This means adding a series of hashtags. One should be the contest name (#DVPit #PitMad #PitProm #PitDark, etc.) Others will help refine the genre, audience, or demographics of your book.
  - o Examples: #YA (Young Adult), #A (Adult), #F (Fantasy), #SF (Science Fiction), #MG (Middle Grade), #Th (Thriller)
  - o Tags allow agents to search for pitches they might be the most interested in without having to read them all.
  - o Each contest has its own rules regarding length, tagging, frequency of, etc.

Common Rules:
- o **Don't "like" other pitches.** Others may retweet your pitch, but the "Like" function is reserved only for agents/publishers. The author will see that and think they've gotten a request from an agent but be crestfallen when they see it's not an agent.

- **If you like another pitch, retweet it!** Spreading the word helps a pitch. Those authors might see your retweet and retweet your pitch in thanks. It can help to build followers, make connections, or just be a cool person on Twitter.
- **Pin your pitch.** Pin your pitch tweet at the top of your page during the contest. This makes it easier for other authors to retweet.
- **If you get a "Like" from an agent, hurray!** Okay, now that your heart has calmed down a little, spend some time checking out the agent or the small press. Do they have a website? Read their website. If not, why are they in an online pitch contest? Would they be a good fit for you to work with?
- **Contact that agent.** If it seems like a good fit, then see if they have a list of requirements for queries from the contest. They might want a particular subject line, a call out in the query letter, etc.

Querying can be frustrating, but there are ways to break down the process into manageable chunks. By creating a strong query letter, there is a better chance of getting the attention of an agent. Once you have an agent, you have a better chance of getting a publisher.

CHAPTER TWENTY: SUBMISSIONS

So, you've spent over a hundred hours writing, honing, and editing your masterpiece, your magnus opus, your precious. Now what?

Now you have a decision to make. Well, you have lots of decisions to make, but first this one.

Traditional publishing or self-publishing?

This was not easy for me to decide. Granted, seven years ago, the view of self-publication was different than it is now. It was still looked on with some disregard then, though that's mostly dropped away. However, I also didn't know what the hell I was doing. I also was very lucky in that I had a friend who also happened to be a small-press publisher.

So, I submitted my book to her, and she published it.

Not everyone is that lucky, nor does everyone want to publish with a small press. Some have a dream of traditional publishing while others crave the control of self-publishing.

There is no wrong decision!

However, as an Extreme Planner, I've discovered something after having ten novels published with a small press. I've discovered that I would much rather have the control of self-publishing, so that's what I'm pursuing with my novels going forward.

For those that do decide to go towards the traditional path, though, this section is for you.

TO AGENT OR NOT TO AGENT

Let's start with some terms so we have a common starting point

- Literary agent—an individual who legally represents your manuscript to a publisher with the goal of seeking the best terms possible for you, the author.
- Query—a letter (normally an email these days) initially sent to a literary agent, trying to get them to represent you.
- Simultaneous (simo) submission – an author submitting to more than one agent or publisher at a time. Most agents will mention on their website if they do not accept simo submissions (most do). If the agency does not accept simo submissions, they will often give you a timeframe to get back with you. If, after that time frame, they do not respond, it's generally understood that you can begin querying other agents. **Note:** even those agents and publishers who accept simultaneous submission request that you let them know if you've accepted a contract elsewhere.

- Slush Pile – The pile of unread manuscripts and queries every agent collects.
- Unsolicited/Solicited Query – An unsolicited query is one sent without a prior request or relationship between the author and the agent. Solicited is when an agent requests a submission, such as when you meet one at a conference or a pitch day on Twitter.
- AAR – Association of Authors Representatives—a professional association of literary agents who uphold certain ethical values while representing you.

BEFORE YOU BEGIN QUERYING

It is expected that when you begin querying, your manuscript is complete and "publication ready;" i.e., content editing, copyediting, and proof editing are complete. This will be future editing by your literary agent/publisher, but you should consider it ready to go once you begin sending out requests. You'll want the manuscript ready to send as soon as you get a positive response from an agent.

WHAT IS A QUERY?

A query is a one-page letter sent to either a literary agent or a publisher to entice them to consider representing your manuscript to a publisher. The query itself should be short, sweet, and to the point. It's a form of targeted marketing that tells your book's story.

WHY DO I NEED A LITERARY AGENT?

If you are not self-publishing, you will more than likely need an agent to represent your work to a publisher.

Most major book publishers and many smaller but substantial publishers will not accept your manuscript directly. While there are some independent literary agents out there, most agents work for a literary agency.

Once an agent agrees to represent your work, and you've signed a contract with them, your agent will then submit your manuscript to publishers they believe will like your book and try to secure a publication deal. They will act as an advocate in both getting your book in front of publishers and helping create an equitable relationship and contract if and when your book is accepted by the publisher.

While some publishers don't require an agent, the query letter works for them directly as well.

FINDING AN AGENT

Find the books similar to your own and see if you can find who agented them. Sometimes that's easy; sometimes not so much.
- Writers Digest Annual Guide to Literary Agents—published around September of each year.
- AgentQuery.com – about 1,000 listings and resource community
- Publisher's Marketplace: publishersmarketplace.com

- Writer's Market: www.writersmarket.com – 400-600 agent listings ($5.99 monthly subscription fee)
- Manuscript Wish List gives what each agent is looking for, searchable by genre: mswishlist.com
- QueryTracker.net – 200 publishers, 1000 agents.
- Absolute Write Water Cooler – list of "editors and predators" https://absolutewrite.com/forums/forumdisplay.php?22-Bewares-Recommendations-amp-Background-Check
- Are they looking for your genre?
- What is their sales track record (often listed on MSWL and other places)? New agents are easier to get in with, but may not have the experience or contacts.
- Does their website look professional and geared toward readers? If it's geared more toward authors, they may be looking to make money off of "reading fees" or "editing packages" rather than sales of your books.
- Do the covers of other books they publish look professional? The agent/publisher usually has control over cover art. If they are crap, they're cutting corners on such costs. This won't help you much. Despite popular belief, people really do judge books by their covers.
- Your agent should be a mentor, coach, cheerleader, and business manager, at least in part. It's their job to market your work to the publisher. It's a partnership.
- Read every contract carefully. Be aware of costs flowing FROM the author. Reputable agents don't ask for cash up front.

AGENT EXERCISE: Research your favorite authors, and see if you can find which agents they use. Make a list of ten agents you would like to work with. Also, make a list of three publishers you'd like to work with.

You want the agent that will work best with you, which means you want one that works with your genre.

Hint: You likely won't get your first choice. You may not even get your twentieth choice. Getting an agent's attention and their representation is, in some ways, harder than writing the book itself.

Extreme Planners like me keep a spreadsheet of the agency name, the agent, their genre, their terms (answer within 6 weeks, etc.) and the date of submission to them. Then I color code those that have responded. That way I can instantly check on the status of all my submissions.

Then you wait.

And wait some more.

Receive your first round of rejections. Refine your query. Send more queries to other literary agents. Note: You *will* get rejected. A lot. Shrug it off. If misery loves company—nearly all major books have been rejected a lot. Harry Potter was rejected. Stephen King's Carrie was rejected multiple times. The Diary of Anne Frank was rejected.

I make it a game to collect a certain amount of rejections. If I reach, say, fifty in a year, that means I've put my work out there fifty times, which I count as a win.

- Refine your letter.
- Send more queries. Make it a game, trying to collect fifty rejections in a year. That way you win either way!
- Repeat last two steps.

- If and when an agent is intrigued, they will ask for a "full" or "partial" manuscript, with details. Send them exactly as they request—no more, no less.
- Wait some more while they evaluate it.
- The agent either sends you a rejection or an acceptance.
  - A rejection can be: "No, go away" or "No, not right now, maybe another book later." This latter means they like your style, but this book isn't right for them right now. Try again with your next book.
  - Most common are "boilerplate" rejections. "I just didn't fall in love with the book."
  - An acceptance will likely come with some suggested revisions. It is up to you how much revision you are willing to do. If the suggested revisions change your style or voice more than you wish, you can decline and keep trying elsewhere.
- Once acceptance and revision are done, the agent will then submit your manuscript to different publishers.
- Oh, look! More waiting.
- The agent may not be able to successfully place your book. If so, you will have in your contract, your options to move to another agent, if you wish.
- If your book is accepted by a publisher, congratulations! You win! More revisions to come!

PREPARE YOUR MANUSCRIPT

I first go through and do one last read-through for errors or inconsistencies. Since many of my novels are set in historical

Ireland, I create a glossary/pronunciation guide in the back for any words that would be unfamiliar to readers. If there's a map, I add it. I write my dedication and/or acknowledgements. I make sure my blurb and taglines are up to date, relevant, and pack some punch.

> Format your submission per the precise guidelines of the publisher you are targeting.

This is very important. If they want triple-spaced, comic sans type size 18, then that's what you do (while cringing so hard your face hurts). More likely it's double-spaced, Times New Roman, size 12. Pay attention to what they want in the manuscript; title in the upper left of each page, author name in the right? No author name in the manuscript, only in the query letter?

CHAPTER TWENTY-ONE: ACCEPTANCE AND MORE EDITING

Acceptance is what brings us together today. Acceptance, that blessed arrangement, that dream within a dream.

As a creative person, one must develop a thick skin for rejection.

> Take each rejection and add it to your armor,
> until you are a titan, invincible!

Oh, sorry. Back to acceptance.

As I mentioned before, I have a small-press publisher, and we have established a relationship. That means while I still submit each book in the series to them (they have a right-of-first-refusal for books in that series in our contract), but unless my quality falls off considerably, they probably won't reject. The most they'll do is ask for significant rewrites, as series are better together.

However, if you are a first-time submitter, it's good to have a plan for when you get that acceptance.

The acceptance will usually come with a contract. Read the contract. Yes, all of it. Even if you have no legal background. Most book contracts are less than five pages and aren't super-difficult. If you are still confused, though, several organizations are out there to help authors evaluate their contracts. I'm a member of the SFWA (Science Fiction Writers Association) and they offer a contract review service. Writer's Relief, a good resource in itself, offers a list of organizations. https://writersrelief.com/writers-associations-organizations/

There are some norms within the industry to be aware of. Make certain there is a time limit to your contract. A common term is five years, after which the rights to your book return to you. In addition, a shorter limit, say, six months, that if the publisher doesn't actually publish your book, the rights revert to you. Ensure they address print, ebook, and audiobook rights, as well as international distribution. The industry standard is to calculate the royalty on the list price (the price it sells for) rather than the net costs, but some small-press publishers still include the latter.

Of course, that doesn't mean the journey is over. Not by a long chalk.

Next comes the edits, the book cover, the blurb, the taglines, the marketing, the cover reveal, the release date, the promotions, and then more promotions. And more marketing. And more marketing, and maybe a few promotions here and there. (No, marketing and promotion are not the same).

So, what do I do now? Other than read the contract, sign it, fill out the cover art questionnaire, the blurb, and the tagline information…?

I wait.

Yup, just like I was waiting after I submitted the book. Now it's waiting on my fantastic editor to read the book and suggest her first round of edits. But that's the subject of the next chapter.

In the meantime, I'm editing book five in the series, Misfortune of Song. While I'm waiting on beta readers to get back to me on that, I've started research on book six, Misfortune of Time. Just started, mind you, but it's begun percolating in my brain. I've already fleshed out the one-paragraph description into five paragraphs, and will end up around three pages before I start defining my characters.

Once the first round of edits were submitted and read, I got a second round. These consisted mostly minor items and questions, more grammatical and stylistic than story questions. I sent those back in good order (plus a couple more refinements I had thought of since my last submission).

The bare truth is that a writer never finishes editing a book. They simply stop being able to make those edits into the final copy.

> "Art is never finished, only abandoned." — da Vinci

When the second round of edits are back to my editor, she could send a third round if needed. However, she didn't – so she sent it on to my publisher. My publisher then sends the manuscript to a proofreader for any final grammatical or punctuation issues. Once that is done, the publisher formats the final form, including title page, dedications, forewords, appendices, back matter, copyright page, etc.

Also during this time is the cover art creation. My publisher works with a fantastic cover artist who has been kind enough to work on most of my book covers. But I don't work directly with her. Normally, all correspondences go through my publisher. It keeps diva authors from pissing off the artist, which is totally understandable. Also, the publisher gets the final say, even though mine is great at taking my input and suggestions.

However, if you work with a large traditional publisher, most of the stories I've heard say that the author has very little input into the cover art. The cover artist doesn't read your book (impossible to do that for all the books!) and is given a cover art information guide. You might be asked to fill this out, or your editor does, or someone else at the publisher. Regardless, you probably won't get a final say on the artwork. This is another reason I'm moving toward self-publishing. That control thing – I want to say what's on my covers. Since I'm also an artist, I'm having fun making my own.

Then the madness begins!

CHAPTER TWENTY-TWO: ARTIST PACKAGE, ARCS, AND REVIEW REQUESTS, OH, MY!

Once the editing, formatting, and cover art is done, the publisher will send me my Author's Kit. This will include several sizes of my book cover, a twitter banner, ARCs (Advanced Reader Copies) of my novel to send to reviewers in .ePub, .mobi, and .PDF form.

This piece of precious gold usually comes about six to eight weeks before publication day, depending on the publisher, of course. You now have all the tools you need to blast the first huge news. Your book is available to the world!

Well, sort of. It's available for pre-order on sites like Amazon, Smashwords, Barnes & Noble, or wherever your publisher has a presence. You have a link to share to everyone. You have ARC copies that you can send out to potential reviewers. You can set up your ad campaigns with the above tools.

I have a whole list of steps to do when I get my Artists' Package. Of course, I do! Otherwise, I wouldn't be a very good Extreme Planner, would I?

- I buy my own book to get the rank "primed" on Amazon. It won't rank you until it registers the first sale, which can take several hours, sometimes a day. But since my books are listed as $0.99 on pre-order, I am willing to spend that just to see it finally with a rank.

- I set up my newsletter announcement. I send out a newsletter once a month.
- I create a blog post, and then share this across Facebook, Twitter, LinkedIn, Instagram, etc.
- I add my book to Goodreads and post an author review there. (Find out if your publisher will add your book to Goodreads to avoid duplication).
- I add book to my Author's Central Page on Amazon. This is an Amazon feature where they will list all the books by a single author. You have to create a sign-in and request to add your books. You can add additional data to your book's page and watch your book rank change from day to day in graph format.
- I add my book to my BookBub page and set up a New Release request.
- I add new book cover everywhere – banners, logos, Facebook pages, Twitter banner, website footers, blog footer, etc.
- I set up ads for the next two months of pre-order.
    - There are hundreds of places out there to advertise your book. Some are free, most are not.
    - BookBub is the Holy Grail. I've never spoken to a single author who regrets getting a BookBub Featured Deal. But they are heavily curated (difficult to obtain) and expensive. Keep trying every month.

- - Other good ones that consistently provide results for me include Ereader News Today and Fussy Librarian.
  - Facebook ads are useful but can get very expensive if they aren't well-targeted.
  - Amazon ads are also useful, though they don't eat through your money as fast. Both types take some time/fiddling to target properly.
  - Each genre has their best ad vendors, and they change regularly.
- I spread the promotions across a series of dates, so that something is happening each day up to the day my book goes back to "normal" price after release.
- I keep a spreadsheet of what is required, as in, some need 5-10 Amazon reviews, some allow new releases, some are just for scifi/fantasy books, etc.
- I send review requests to my reviewer list. This is a separate mailing list I keep with people who have specifically requested to be part of my ARC or beta reader team.
- I announce on various forums, such as AWWC (Absolute Write Water Cooler).
- I send an announcement to my local community arts newsletter.
- I set up a blog tour/Review Blitz.
- I submit for awards at various places.
- I set up a Facebook Release Party or Cover Reveal Party.
- I post the pre-order information on Facebook book/author pages.

- I post the pre-order information on Facebook special interest pages (Ireland, Celtic, Pagan, History, etc.)
- I arrange for author interviews or blog swaps.
- I record the opening scene on video to post to my YouTube channel.
- I create a video book trailer and post to my YouTube channel, Facebook, and Twitter.

The above list takes me at least a full 8-10 hours. Yes, that's a lot of work, and the release isn't even here yet! However, other than shouting the news at the rooftop, there's more effort spent now than there is when the actual release occurs.

This is an ongoing process. The first time, it can be quite scary. Just take each step one at a time. After a few book releases, it becomes a checklist.

> Writing a book is not a one-and-done thing.
> It's like raising a child.
> Just because the kid is about to move out to college doesn't mean your responsibilities are finished!

PART FIVE: SELF-PUBLISHING PATH

CHAPTER TWENTY-THREE: FORMATTING HELL

If you decide to self-publish, then the previous chapter is mostly irrelevant, after you've got the editing done.

However, self-publishing starts a whole new set of things you must do. Extreme Planning is helpful here, as well as being a control freak, some detail-oriented obsession, and lots of time, especially the first time around, for learning the process.

Because a self-published author basically does everything themselves, that means you need to learn the following skills, or be prepared to pay someone to do them for you.

- More editing (yes, a final polish. Trust me, there are still typos in there)
    - Side note: Even trad published professional books have typos. But a good rule of thumb is to have fewer than one per 3,000 words
- Formatting (for ebook and print book, interior and exterior)
- Cover Art (for ebook, print book, and audiobook)
- Audiobook
- Publishing to various platforms

- Promotion
- Getting reviews

Now, promotion and getting reviews would be your responsibility whether you self-publish or go traditional, but a traditional publisher would take some of the burden from you as an author. That doesn't mean they'll do everything, unless you are Stephen King or James Patterson, but they can do some of it. Since you likely are not (if Stephen King is actually reading my little book on Extreme Planning, I would let out such a huge fan squee he would hear it in Maine! And then probably write a best-selling horror book about the awful sound). then you need to learn how to promote yourself.

The next chapters will address each one of these areas.

FINAL EDITING/PROOFREADING

Because you are self-publishing, you cannot rely on your publisher to give your manuscript a final, professional edit. This is an area where you should not skimp, and professional editing/proofreading can make the difference between readers considering your work amateur rather than professional.

FORMATTING

As a self-pub author, you have lots of decisions to make. At the moment, you need to decide what formats to offer your book in.

- Ebook: The easiest to format, but usually the lowest price point

- Print: There's still a huge market for print books, but they have a higher price point and a lower profit. Also, you risk getting stuck with lots of unsold print copies
- Audiobook: a booming market, but requires a lot of work on top of what you've already done. (Audiobook production is covered in a later chapter)

What to include:

Of course, you want to include the actual meat of the book, but there are other items to include in your final proof. For instance, you'll want to start with a title page, a copyright notice, and any dedications, forewords, or acknowledgements. You might have a pronunciation guide, map, list of major characters, or prologue to increase your reader's immersion into your world.

After your manuscript, you may have an epilogue, an author's note, a section about the author, a listing of your other books, and perhaps a preview of another book, which can be an excellent marketing tool. You may also wish to thank your readers and request they leave a review.

Once you have all these sections compiled into your draft, you'll need to format it.

eBook

You will need to adjust your formatting depending on what publishing platform you choose, but you will, at a minimum, need to format the book consistently and convert into an electronic format.

Note: Lulu, Draft2Digital, and Smashwords only require a .doc or .docx document, and will convert from that to the other formats.

- .mobi: Mobi or Mobipocket is the format that Amazon's Kindle readers use. Some of the Kindle models will also read other formats, but this is by far the most common for these readers. Nook, however, doesn't read this type of file.
- .ePub: Nook, Androids, Kindle Fire, and most other devices will read .ePub formats.
- PDF: Most anything can read on a PDF, but you lose the ability for pages to shift based on the screen size, a huge advantage to dedicated readers and phones.
- Note: Lulu, Draft2Digital, and Smashwords only require a .doc or .docx document, and will convert from that to the other formats.

There are other formats, but these are the primary ones most people create their books in. In order to properly format the interior of the book, you'll have to use a converting program. There are lots out there.

A converting program will take your manuscript from a Word document and format it into the necessary ebook forms. Some are very basic, some are more complex. The basic ones offer few options for personalizing your book, but the complex ones require some learning curve to understand them. For any of these, check with your local library, as they may have copies on their computers.

- Calibre: Free from KDP (Kindle Direct Publishing) Basic with few options. You can upload a Word .doc or .docx file.
- Jutoh: A few more options than Calibre.
- Vellum: Most people agree Vellum is great. However, it has a few drawbacks, including only being available for Mac. While you can use it in a Mac simulator, I tried this and found it clunky for my tastes. It's pretty expensive, though, $$$$.
- InDesign: Part of the Adobe Suite, this is incredibly flexible with lots of options. It also has a very steep learning curve. I've used Photoshop for decades, and it still took me all day to figure out how to format my book for print. Even for the second book, its quirks meant it took me four hours. However, I have it exactly how I want it. Cost $ BUT that's per month.
- Scrivener: Primarily a drafting tool with great organization functions, it also offers digital formatting options, but no print formatting. Cost about $$.
- Word: Word, while highly popular for writing the manuscript, doesn't allow for ebook formatting. It's print formatting is also unadvisable.
- Reedsy: Free but again, with limited options.
- More options pop up all the time, so do some research. Read the reviews. Find out what's most important to you. Short learning curve? Cost? More options?

Once you've chosen your software, you have other decisions to make.

- Will you have left-justified or right-justified text (leaving a ragged edge to your columns), or full-justified, like newspaper columns? Check the top sellers in your genre to check what the standard is.
- Will you allow hyphenation of words to aid that full justification, or prefer wide spacing for shorter lines?
- What font should you use? Most ereaders allow the reader to change their font. For print reading, serif fonts have been more common in the past. You might use the same font from your book cover art on the title page, but other than that, keep it simple to one font throughout for the text, and perhaps one for the chapter titles.
- Do you want an image for scene breaks instead of the traditional ### or ***?
- Do you want a drop cap at the beginning of each chapter? A drop cap is the large initial capital letter that takes up 2-3 lines of space and is used in several genres in traditional publishing. Some of the above programs allow for that, but some do it poorly.
- Most eBook formatting platforms will help you create a linkable table of contents. Some of them are less user friendly and require a lot of fixing for their automatic linking.
- Page numbers? Pretty much useless for ereaders, but print copies will need this decision made. Top? Bottom? Middle? Right/left? Starting page one on the first page of Chapter One, rather than the front matter is standard.

- Headers/Footers – if you are formatting a non-fiction book or have some inline notes, these are important.

Once you have your eBook cover art complete and your interior format finished, you can upload your eBook to your distributor(s) of choice.

Print

Print books require all of the above decisions plus a few more.

Why, in this day and age, would an author want to go through the trouble and expense of having print copies? Several reasons. First, not everyone likes reading eBooks. Many people still love to read print copies. Second, libraries still request print copies. While they also carry eBooks to borrow, if you want books available in libraries, you should offer a print option. Third, it's much easier to get your books into local bookstores if you have prints. Fourth, if you attend any author events, it's much easier to sign and sell print copies in person. Most platforms such as IngramSpark, Amazon, and Lulu, offer print on demand, so you can print only the number of books you want.

Some of the above software platforms do not format for print, as they are ebook only. Reedsy, InDesign, and Vellum all have print options. Do some research before you commit, if you are looking to have print copies.

Additional concerns for print formatting:
- You must determine your trim size, or how big you want your final book to be. I prefer 6"X9", but there are several options. Keep in mind that the larger the book, the fewer the pages, and most print platforms calculate their printing costs by the page.
- Avoid widows and orphans, single lines left over from a paragraph on the bottom or top of pages.
- Check any unusually hyphenated words, especially proper nouns.
- Pay attention to what pages are on the left and the right. Your Title page should be on the right, after a blank page. Your chapters should start on the right.
- Revisit your justification choices. Is full justification still working? Or is left better? If you are fully justifying, check for those odd paragraphs where the last line is stretched across.
- Check the number of spaces before each chapter title for consistency
- Double-spaced or single-spaced? Maybe 1.5?
- What size font should you use?
- Make certain the font you use is licensed for print and ebooks.
- If you had hyperlinks in your eBook, consider writing out the HTML for the print version, as hyperlinks won't be useful on the page.
- What color and weight paper will you use?
- You will also need to create a wrap-around cover that includes your spine and back cover, as the ebook only requires a front.

This adds another dimension, as you must calculate how large an area to give your spine based on the number of pages. Both KDP and IngramSpark have calculators to create templates for wrap-around covers to help you create them properly.
- Will you use a matte or glossy cover?
- Make sure to create your front and back matter; copyright page, dedication, thank you page, other books by page, preview for another book, about the author, etc.

Once you have your cover art and your formatted interior, you can then upload both files to your distributor of choice. I highly recommend ordering a proof copy before you go live, to ensure your formatting for both interior and exterior works the way you intended.

As an Extreme Planner, I have extensive checklists with each of the above points for each of my books. It helps me remember the niggling details and avoiding a horrific discovery of skipping one later, after I'm already at an author signing and noticing the font on my title page is off.

CHAPTER TWENTY-FOUR: JUDGING A BOOK BY ITS COVER

"Never judge a book by a cover" just doesn't apply to actual books. People constantly judge by the cover, to the point that it's incredibly important to fuel sales. The cover is your first line of attack to get readers, but a bad cover may keep them from even giving your blurb or first chapter a chance. The point of a cover is to tempt the reader to pick up your book and read the blurb.

While some well-established authors with a dedicated fanbase might get away with slapping together a reasonable cover for the genre, a first-time author cannot afford to be so blasé. The cover must intrigue and ultimately entice the reader to read the blurb.

Unless you are a professional graphic designer, it is usually a mistake to design your own cover. Yes, it's cheaper, and in some genres, you can get away with it. However, most people who think they are graphic designers are not. And I say this as someone who grew up creating art, whose grandmother was an art teacher and whose mother has a Fine Arts degree, earned most of a Fine Arts degree herself, and has still done some cringey cover designs.

But art and cover art aren't the same thing. One has aspects of the other, but there are so many other factors that are required. It's taken me a few years to learn what good cover art looks like. More so, what professional cover art looks like.

There are several things to keep in mind, but first and foremost, the book cover must evoke the genre. If you see a book cover with spaceships on it, with a blocky, sans serif font, in blue and white monochrome color scheme, your first thought is "Space Science Fiction," not "Regency Romance." The cover is the reader's first clue to genre, tone, and theme.

Other elements to keep in mind, whether you're using a designer or doing it yourself (not all designers are created equal):
- Author name AND title clearly written.
- Easily read font that matches your genre (don't use more than one or two, pretty please with sugar on top!)
- Good contrast. If everything is similar in tone (darkness/lightness) then it all melds together and won't pop, especially at thumbnail size.
- Use the front, spine, and back (in print books) to communicate your genre, tone, and story elements. Blurb on the back, perhaps with author information and/or photo.
- Not too busy/confusing. Keep your composition simple and elegant.
- Draw the allegory. Don't try to portray a particular scene but make the image symbolic of the story elements and conflicts.
- Keep your name smaller than the title (unless you're Stephen King).

- No "written by" or "by" – this is only for amateurs. Pros never do it.
- Maybe include a tagline or Editorial Review but keep both short.
- Series name and book number within the series
- Use high PPI (pixels per inch) to avoid fuzzy graphics.
- To trope or not to trope? That's a good question! Study the trends for your genre. The best way is to twist a trope well, but that's also difficult.
- Define target audience and use that definition to drive your cover art choices. Cozy mysteries have different covers than thrillers. Young Adult covers are different from romances.
- Color emotion. Red is great for horror stories. Blue works well for thrillers.
- Title is part of the cover draw. Choose your title carefully. Check Amazon to see if there is already a very popular book by the same name. While titles aren't copyrighted, it can be confusing if you write a book called Twilight or The Stand.
- Choose a font that reflects your genre. Make it legible. While romance books should have a font that reflects it, don't make it so flowery or cursive it's illegible as a thumbnail.
- In your composition, remember the rule of three. Things can be more interesting in the one-third/two-third locations, either horizontally or vertically.
- Not always, though! Sometimes symmetry is powerful, too.
- Keep your proportions reasonable. Try to balance the composition with your title and author name.

- Pay close attention to shading/shadow/light. Where is your light source? Are all the elements lit properly for that? How strong is the light? What color?
- Most amateur covers don't pay enough attention to edges. They paste figures into a scene, but the hard edges scream they don't belong there. Soften them. Blend them.
- Focal Point – Strong, visual lines leading to a point in the distance can draw the reader in.
- Z-formation. Title, diagonal line of artwork on the cover, then author name, all forming a Z.
- Pay attention to the power of extra space/negative space
- Copyright – don't just steal your images from the internet. Either take photos yourself, purchase licenses from stock photo sites, or explore "creative commons" images, those photographs and artwork artists have created and offered for anyone to use, royalty-free. Your book cover can be removed if you are in copyright violation, and Amazon can ban you.

Different artistic techniques:
- Stock image manipulation (cheapest, most common). iStockPhoto, Deposit Photos, Shutterstock, Dreamstime, all sites that have photos and illustrations specifically for graphic artists to use for things like book covers and advertisements. Make certain you're purchasing a license for commercial use.
- Illustration (need pure artistic talent). Illustration is more common in certain genres, like high fantasy or cozy mysteries.

- Bespoke photography (made to order photography). You need to be a photographer with a willing model (if you have a human in your cover art plan).

Typical cost:
- $100-$200 for premade covers (covers already made by a designer for sale as is)
- $200-$500 for a newbie or budget artist
- $500-$800 for an experienced designer
- $800-$1500 for a top-tier designer

Please let me reiterate. Unless you have a background and/or training as an artist, you probably won't want to do your covers for yourself. This is the first thing your readers will see. Many of them make a split-second decision on the book cover art. You will be spending money on advertising to get that book cover in front of their faces. Do you really want to skimp on it? Do you really want to waste lots of money in advertising by using a cover that's unappealing, bland, too confusing, or not genre-specific?

A true Extreme Planner knows their own limitations and works within that knowledge. I do have artistic training. Even with artistic training and talent, book covers are a specific area that requires particular skills.

I have a solid base in art education. I've sold my jewelry, painting, and photography professionally. And my first four book covers were horribly amateur.

If you do decide to try your hand at cover creation, or are working with an artist, keep in mind it's fairly common to go through two or three different concepts before you settle on the one that works best for your story and aesthetic.

> **BOOK COVER EXERCISE:** Search for book covers in your genre. Pick twenty you like and twenty you don't like. Write down the elements of those covers that speak to you, and those that don't. List ways in which you can use these elements to reflect your own novel. Pay attention to color scheme, figures, symbols, lighting, illustration style, font.

CHAPTER TWENTY-FIVE:
TO AUDIO OR NOT TO AUDIO?

Audiobooks are a rising market, and one that deserves some consideration. Many people listen to audiobooks as entertainment as they do other tasks, such as housework or driving. While it requires a great deal of effort, it could be another platform to sell your story.

Creation

Producing an audiobook is difficult and expensive. It has a whole different skill set than writing a book. However, if you are willing to put in the time and effort to learn the process, it can be done.

You have to make a choice, however. Well, you have to make several, but the first choice is if you want to **narrate your own books**? This has both pros and cons.

Pros:
- You don't have to pay a narrator
- You can work at your own pace
- You have complete control over your project

- Author-narrated books are preferred by many listeners

Cons:
- It's incredibly time-consuming
- You have to learn recording and editing
- You need a recording area free of noise and echo
- You may not have a great narrative voice

On the other hand, **hiring a narrator** has its own set of pros and cons.

Pros:
- Typically a higher quality narration
- It's less time-consuming
- You don't have to learn recording and editing
-

Cons:
- It's expensive, either in up-front fees or in royalty shares
    o   Up-front fees often cost over $100 per recorded hour. A 100,000-word novel comes to about 12 hours, so would cost at least $1200 for the narrator.
    o   Both ACX and Findaway Voices offer royalty share programs, where the author and the narrator both receive a share of the royalties in lieu of an up-front fee
- You have to work with someone else's schedule
- Control is less complete

- You have to audition and choose a narrator, and if something goes wrong, you have to do it all over again

Whichever choice you make, that will be up to you, your budget, your level of comfort in learning a new skill set, your voice, etc. However, I will say this. I chose to do my own narration. I learned the technology, set up a recording area, and have now recorded three of my audiobooks. It is exhausting. Just doing a half hour of narration drains you. It's like acting in a play, full of intense voices and emotions. On the other hand, it's immensely satisfying to complete one. I spend about two or three hours for every hour of recorded narration in editing, formatting, and uploading to the various platforms.

Distribution

There are several options of audiobook platforms, but by far the largest is Audible, which is owned by Amazon. Other options include Nook, Chirp, or Google Audiobooks. There are also distribution platforms that combine many of these networks, such as Findaway Voices. I personally use both Audible (ACX) and Findaway Voices and ensure neither are marked "exclusive." Unlike print and eBooks, it's much more cumbersome to sell audiobooks on your own site, as you'd need to compile a zip file to transfer the large audio files in a listenable format.

Again, making the audiobook available to libraries is possible through these platforms, and many people consume their audiobooks in this manner. You do get paid for borrowings, just not as much as if you sold an individual audiobook.

> **EXERCISE:** Record yourself reading the first scene of your book. Listen to yourself. Re-record at least twice, so you can find your voice and rhythm. Is this something you'd pay to listen to? Why or why not? Now have someone else listen to it and give you honest feedback. Then go and listen to a few samples of professionally recorded audiobooks. Are you in the same ballpark? Are you in the same continent?

CHAPTER TWENTY-SIX:
SO MANY PUBLISHING PLATFORMS

When you are considering how to deliver your books, there are, once again, many choices to make. As a self-published author, you have all the control, but that also means you have to make all the decisions, and you're the one to suffer for poor research, bad decisions, or just lack of information. You can, on the other hand, paralyze yourself with all the options out there, doing so much research you never actually publish your book. The trick is to do enough research to find your best options, and go for it.

The 400-pound gorilla in the room is, of course, Amazon. They are, by orders of magnitude, the largest book distributor in the world. Being a self-published author and not putting your books on Amazon is a severe shot in the foot. It can be done, but it'll give you a heck of a limp. I don't recommend it unless you know what you're doing and have a very good reason.

Several options are free or low-cost to upload your ebook or print book.

- Amazon

- Lulu
- Kobo
- Barnes & Noble
- IngramSpark
- Draft2Digital (a consolidator that distributes to Amazon, Apple, Barnes & Noble, Kobo, Scribd, SmashWords, OverDrive, and others)
- BookChunnel
- More pop up all the time, so do some research and find some that might work best with your genre

If you opt to have an audiobook, you still have choices:
- ACX (Owned by Audible, thus Amazon)
- Findaway Voices (a consolidator)
- Chirp
- Audiobooks.com

On Amazon and ACX, both have exclusive programs (Kindle Unlimited is the Amazon program) where you get more royalties if you distribute through them alone. For some authors, that's a great deal. KU has a growing platform and certain genres, like romance, work blockbusters on it. However, not all authors or genres want to take that gamble. It means your ebook cannot be distributed anywhere else.

Most distributors will give you royalties from 35-70%, depending on the platform, book price, and exclusivity deal. For instance, Amazon is 70% unless your book is 99c, and then it's only 35%.

If you go through a traditional publisher, though, you may only get half of any royalty. This is one reason many authors are switching to self-publishing.

Each platform has its own formatting requirements for the interior and cover of the book. And the requirements for ebook are different from print. This does require a steep learning curve, though there are services out there if you're interested in outsourcing it. There are also programs to help you with the formatting options.

- Amazon has its own Kindle Create tool (free, but only works for Amazon)
- Vellum (Mac required, small fee)
- Adobe InDesign (powerful tool but very steep learning curve, also the most expensive)
- Scrivener Compile (small fee)
- New software is being created all the time – find one that works with your budget, skill set, learning ability, and comfort level

Once you've created your files, formatted them, checked the formatting, corrected, checked again, corrected the seventh time, you are ready. You can put the ebook up for order, or pre-order, set your release date, and relax.

Well, no, you can't. You have advertising to set up. You need to create your newsletter announcement, post to your blog, create ads in Amazon. Create a Bookbub profile. Upload the book to Goodreads. So many details! But you can relax a little bit. The hardest part is done.

That's a lie.

PART SIX: THE HEADY AFTERMATH

CHAPTER TWENTY-SEVEN: RELEASE THE KRAKEN!

This is it.

This is the day I've been working toward for over a year. The release day of my novel! Of course, this day is rather anticlimactic as, if I am smart, I'll have done most of my work already with the ARCs and review requests, setting up ads, etc.

However, I still need to shout it out from the treetops. I write a blog post, make announcements in various places – my Facebook page, Twitter, LinkedIn, InstaGram, any other social networking platforms. I email my ARC recipients to remind them to please post their reviews. I check on any bloggers that are hosting me today. These are all steps I have listed in my, you guessed it, spreadsheet. Please don't say you're surprised. Extreme Planner, remember?

Then I wait.

Then I refresh that Amazon link, looking for both sales and reviews. And again. And again. Several times per hour. Why isn't it moving? Where are all my reviewers? They promised they'd post on release day! All I hear are crickets. Better refresh again. Argh! Oh, wait! There's my first review, and it's 5 stars, woohoo! And I made more sales.

My publisher said I made 147 sales in pre-order, so the opening day sales aren't huge. I expect that now. Most people who wanted the novel had already bought it. Now they're all reading it (hopefully) and enjoying it (even more hopefully).

My baby has finally left the nest (sniff!). I hope it can fly.

Another review! Two! Two whole reviews! Mwahahahah!

More refreshes. A few more sales trickle in.

That evening, I get ready for my Facebook Release Party. This is an online discussion at a particular time that anyone can join. Often other authors are invited in a "takeover" format, so their fans can become your fans and vice versa. Prizes, discussions, etc. occur. Hilarity and even minor amusement.

Then that's over. Three reviews now, all five-star. Yay! But what happened to the other fifteen people that got ARCs? Some may not be done with the book. Some may never read it. Some may have forgotten. I email them a reminder several days later – one had thought she'd posted a review, and hadn't, so she fixed that right away. Some ghost me, and I never hear from them, so they get crossed off my reviewer list.

Five days after release, I've got six delightful reviews, including one that said those who love Outlander and Mists of Avalon would love my series. Gotta appreciate that!

And now my book goes back up to full price, and I start concentrating on the next novel coming out.

I don't forget about this one, of course. None of your books are ever "done." The promotion and advertising is ongoing. They're like children who have gone off to college, but you still have to bail them out when their car breaks down or they need to do their laundry. They're always your children.

And that's it – the full novel cycle as lived by me, an author who loves to dive in head-first, an Extreme Planner Extraordinaire!

CHRISTY NICHOLAS

CHAPTER TWENTY-EIGHT: BEGGING FOR REVIEWS, OR MORE WAYS TO ALIENATE YOUR FRIENDS AND FAMILY

So, you've written your first draft. You've bled, sweated, and cried to get it professionally edited, published it (either with a publisher or on your own), and now it's out there like a toddler, ready to walk.

Now what?

Now you drink champagne and party all night. No? Well, now you want people to buy your book. Well, okay, maybe do some celebration. Enjoy the moment! Eat the cake! Drink the champagne! But then the next morning inevitably comes. Even if you are picked up by a major publisher, unless you're Stephen King or JK Rowling, your marketing and promotion is up to you. One of the tools of promotion is getting reviews.

WHAT ARE REVIEWS?

Reviews are commentary and judgment from your readers. Some contain mini-summaries of your book, some don't. Some include spoilers. Some just contain "I like it." Some are rude and you wonder if they even read your book (never reply to negative reviews! Take the high road.) All are valuable. Yes, even the negative reviews have value.

A healthy number of reviews (say, over 20) give readers reassurance that your book has a readership, has caught the attention of a decent number of people, and they've cared enough to take the time to leave a review. Most readers do NOT leave reviews. Maybe less than 1% do so. Therefore, it can feel like pulling teeth in order to get reviews. Begging, buying, tricking – there are many ways to get reviews, some allowed, some not.

WHY DO YOU NEED REVIEWS?

Reviews offer a glimpse into the book for those making a decision on whether to buy it. They offer a 3rd-person perspective on its worth. Now, most people looking at reviews for their decision-making realize that everyone has personal bias. However, too many bad reviews (or too many glowing ones!) can indicate something is wrong, either with your book or with the reviews themselves.

Too many bad reviews: There might be something wrong. Either you are marketing to the wrong group of readers, or your editing needs more work, or your story line isn't as tight as it could be, or you've something else that might need adjusting. Another possibility is that you've pissed someone off and they've started a bad-review campaign against you, using their friends. Don't laugh – it used to be common. That's one reason Amazon has tightened the strictures against reviewers. Many readers will look at the worst reviews to see if the reason for the bad review is something they care about. For instance, if a poor review says there were too many instances of violence or taking God's name in vain, I might gloss over that. However, if it mentions horrible editing, I might hesitate. Or if it mentions something that I don't wish to deal with, like gory violence.

Too many good reviews: Yes, it's a thing. It looks suspicious if you have all 5-star reviews or even none under 4-stars. Especially if Amazon starts investigating to see if you're getting reviews from friends and family.

Several advertisers require a minimum number and/or star value to your Amazon reviews in order to accept your book for advertising. The most notorious of these is Bookbub, but some smaller ones also require it. Bookbub doesn't have a set minimum, but common wisdom is the more, the better.

I would say about 50 is the magic mark for Bookbub. I had 54 on one book before I got my first featured deal with them. However, another book had 153 before I got a Bookbub deal on that one, and I've gotten a deal for a book with only 22, so there is no true magic mark.

However, I think getting reviews on Bookbub itself is also important to them. They are growing their platform and getting both followers and reviews there must help that.

FROM WHOM/HOW DO YOU GET THEM?

Your fans, of course! What, you don't have any? Well, get some!

Seriously, though, getting reviews from readers is like pulling teeth. No matter how many times you nudge them or ask for the review at the back of the book (do this), not even 1% of readers will leave a review. Amazon has strict rules on reviews (see below), as well, and may pull the review if they believe it to violate these rules. Worse, if they determine you are buying reviews, they can yank your book and ban you. Yup!

Some sources below are online magazines or industry review groups. Some of these are free, some have a cost.
- InD'Tale Magazine
- Discovering Diamonds
- Night Owl Romance
- Historical Novel Society
- The Wishing Shelf

I have a list of reviewers I ask for each new book. When I get the ARC (Author Review Copy) from my publisher, I send out my requests. Don't wait until your book is out! You want some to post the day of release, if possible.

There are bloggers who do book reviews for free, but most have a long waiting list or specific genres. It's a long, tedious process asking for them, but it's worth it. This website lists a huge amount of reviewers by category with a link to submission guidelines. Some might be out of date, but you should find plenty of options. http://www.theindieview.com/indie-reviewers/

Review Tour: You can also organize (or have a service organize) a review blitz, which is essentially a "tour" of several review bloggers. Either on release day or several days, depending on the organizer. This gets the buzz out about your book over several platforms and offers the reviewers content. Usually the service costs about $100, and while they can never guarantee a certain number of reviews, several are reliable. I recommend a few, including Goddess Fish Productions and Itsy Bitsy Book Bits as services I've used in the past.

Newsletter: I have an author newsletter, but I have a smaller group of newsletter members for those who wish to beta read or review ARC copies of my books. Yes, I give them a free copy, and ask that they leave a review (not require – ask!). This is a much smaller subset of my larger reader group, and if I send one for a review and they don't leave one, I simply don't send them one the next time. Simple as that. If you have beta readers or ARC readers, ask them to leave reviews. They've already invested time and effort into the book and (especially if you've thanked them in your acknowledgements) are part of this project.

Author Street Team: Another technique is getting an Author Street Team together. These are a few devoted fans (almost like a fan club!) who will share the word of your new releases, post reviews, etc.

Facebook Groups: There are a few Facebook groups out there that are for reviewing books, such as Fantasy & Romance Review Group, Books/ARCs for Review, Booksgosocial Book Review Club. Each one has rules, and you should follow them.

Endorsement reviews: These are reviews from other authors. You see them on the traditionally published books, like Diana Gabaldon giving a review for Naomi Novik's book. These are hard to get from named authors. Usually, traditionally published authors are under contract to only give such reviews as per their own publisher's request. However, you might get them from lower-tier authors. Develop friendships with them and ask!

Editorial reviews: These are paid reviews (which means they do not get posted in the Amazon Review section) from a supposedly prestigious service that you can post in the information section of your book or even on your cover. Example: "USA Today says 'A thrilling ride'" on the cover of a Grisham novel).

Some Editorial Review sources include Kirkus and City Book Review (San Francisco, Manhattan). These usually cost a big chunk of money, but do hold some cache, as they are picky about which books they choose. Your mileage may vary.

WHERE DO YOU WANT THEM?

The most popular platform, though not the only one, is Amazon. There is a reason for this. It's the single largest platform for buying online books in the world. Also, some advertisers require a minimum number of reviews and stars to allow you to advertise with them. It's believed that the holy grail of advertising, Bookbub, requires a decent amount of Amazon reviews before they'll accept your book for a featured deal. I have thoughts on this later.

Review platforms:
- Amazon
- Bookbub
- Goodreads
- Smashwords
- Barnes & Noble/Nook
- LibraryThing
- Book Riot
- Bookish
- Booklist

Amazon has several rules on what NOT to do (see below). Other platforms aren't as picky, but Amazon is the standard most authors try to comply with.

HOW DO YOU *NOT* GET REVIEWS?

These are against Amazon rules (which change without notice):
- Paid reviews (including a free book in exchange for a review, i.e., quid pro quo)
- Reviews by close family or friends (how it determines this is a matter of much debate. However, trolling through Facebook/Goodreads friends is a possibility, so better not to leave those linked. Amazon owns Goodreads).

- Review swaps - If I review Author A and Author A reviews me, both reviews may be flagged and removed, especially if they are close together in time.

    While this is a relatively short list, each item has lots of implications and gray areas. How does Amazon judge who your "close family and friends" are? Can review swaps be done if the reviews are months apart, i.e., I review Author A in January and she picks up my book in April and reviews it? Unknown. The most inscrutable part of Amazon is they will send a message to the reviewer saying the review violates their rule – but not which rule or how. The appeal process is also opaque and long.

CHAPTER TWENTY-NINE: SELLING YOURSELF

It's time for everyone's favorite subject: Marketing.

Once you're done groaning, I'll continue. No, I'll wait.

Marketing, advertising, and promotion (yes, they are very different things) can sound like dirty words to authors. Authors tend to be creative types, those more in the world of their own imagination, while the disciplines of marketing, advertising, and promotion are firmly in the business world. People make careers of the latter, and it's a difficult world for an amateur to grasp.

As I'm an accountant, I've taken classes in marketing. I enjoyed it, especially the artistic aspects. However, it's a difficult discipline to master if you don't have a background in it.

On the other hand, it's an absolutely essential part of self-publishing. A bit of a Catch-22. Self-publishing means you must learn several different disciplines unrelated to actually writing a book. Editing, cover art, audiorecording… and marketing.

While an intensive course on marketing is well outside the scope of this book, I can give you some pointers and hints to form a plan, as well as some resources to dive more deeply into the discipline.

Let's start with some definitions and examples.

> Marketing: This is the overall discipline of researching and analyzing the
> competition, pricing, and demographics.

- This is where you examine other book covers in your genre to figure out what elements your own should have, what platforms might work with your book, and who you want to target your advertising to.
    - Your genre, urban fantasy, appeals 57% to women and 43% to men.
    - There are distinct markets for Young Adult Urban Fantasy and Adult Urban Fantasy (Buffy the Vampire Slayer vs. Highlander)
    - Most urban fantasy covers portray a young person with some sort of power object in their hand (ball of fire, lightning, sword, crossbow) standing in a city scene. Common color schemes include blue, purple, green, dark/night theme.

> Advertising: The actual message going out to your customers, no matter the platform.

- Advertising asks the customer to buy your product. You can have both free and paid advertising.
    - Amazon ads/Amazon book page
    - Social media ads such as on Facebook, Twitter, Instagram, BookBub
    - Press release

> Promotions: Non-advertising communications that talk about your product.

- These don't specifically say "buy my book" but raise the awareness of you and your work.
    - Blog posts about the culture your book is set in
    - Video interview with the author
    - Newsletter with author news, excerpts, book discount information

Some resources I've found to navigate the labyrinthine world of advertising include Reedsy, Ads for Authors, Writer's Digest, Writing Excuses, and the Self-Publishing Show Podcast. These range from free to very expensive. However, the items on the expensive side are very worth it, and full of intense, step-by-step information on how to create, modify, refine, and maintain ads on the more difficult-to-navigate platforms such as Amazon and Facebook. They also have resources on creating your book covers, writing ad copy, and BookBub ads.

There is a multitude of free and paid advertising options for authors. Some are worth crap. Others are worth gold. It can be difficult to discover which works, and certain things will work wonderful for one author or genre and be horrible for another. Unfortunately, this becomes a matter of trial and error, and if you are on a tight budget, paid advertising can be difficult. The free options also take trial and error.

FREE!

Free advertising is great, but you usually get what you pay for. This is why promotion is so important. A lot of promotion can be done for free. Newsletters, social media presence, websites, interviews, blog posts, etc. can raise your profile, create buzz, and inform your potential readers, all before you've even published a book. You can find creative venues, such as recording a video of you reading your first chapter for YouTube, or running a contest for a free ebook on social media.

PAID

I find the gold standard in author advertising is still BookBub. This platform has hundreds of thousands of avid readers, by genre, and their Featured Deals have always paid off for me. However, they have high standards on which books they will run, and it can be difficult to get a Featured Deal. I tried for two years before I got one. Now I get them fairly frequently and they are always worth it. They cost a lot, depending on if you do a U.S. or International-only deal, and which genre you are in, it can be anywhere from $200 to $1000. But I have never lost money on one.

Other good places for my books have been Ereader News Today (also difficult to get in but not nearly as much as BookBub), FreeBooksy/BargainBooksy, eBook Soda, and FKBT (Free Kindle Books & Tips). As I said before, these may not work for all authors or genres, but they work for me. Your mileage may vary.

Many advise that you should "Step" your promotions, especially for your book release. This involves having different promos on different days as you lead up to the release date. That way, you not only build on each promotion's success, but you can determine which are the more powerful, effective venues for your work. This will help you decide which to use for the next one, or when you have a sale. I have tried step promotions, but it's difficult to say if this is more or less effective without control group experiments.

NEWSLETTERS

One of the most effective ways of (mostly) free promotion I've used is a robust newsletter. Newsletters can scare many authors, especially at the beginning, but it's a wonderful resource. The trick is to write one at least every month, as studies show that readers want to hear from their subscribed authors at least that often. But what if you don't have new content every month? Not to worry! Here are some tricks.

- Trivia about your book setting – I do a "Celtic Corner" feature in each issue. Something about Irish history or language, a place I've visited, "This day in History" can all be a bit of interesting knowledge about the world you write in.
- News on your books – even if you don't have anything published yet, you can let your readers know where you are on various projects. For example, right now I have Taming of the Few with a second round of beta readers, Extreme Planning in first draft, and Much Ado About Dying in first draft. I have one book on sale and another coming up. Here are the links!
- Other authors' books that are similar to yours in genre or theme – there are author newsletter swap sites where you can find other authors with books in similar genre.
- Free excerpt from something you are working on or something you've published. This is especially great for your readers. I put this at the bottom so readers have to go through the rest to get to the good stuff.
- A listing of all your books including the buy links at the end.
- I use Mailerlite, but there are several options out there, including Mailchimp, ConstantComment and others. I say "mostly" free above, because while these are free or low-cost at

a certain level of subscribers, they start costing monthly when you get more readers. This is also a reason to "curate" your list and unsubscribe those readers who never open your newsletters after six months or so.

- I set up a free short story for new subscribers, using BookFunnel. I also send them another story after a week, after a month, and after two months. Everyone loves free! I can set up an automatic 'flowchart' in MailerLite for this process.
- There are give-away services that let you build your newsletter subscribers by running a contest with, say, twenty other authors. Everyone gets one book free, two or three winners get all books free, and maybe a solid prize like an Amazon gift card or a kindle. These are great for building your subscribers, BUT you may end up with a bunch of subscribers only in it for the freebies. A mixed blessing. I consider this useful to build your platform, but then when you get bigger, you can refine and curate your list.
- Have a sign up page, or a Q-code, at any in-person author readings or signings you do! Word of mouth advertising at its finest.

PERSONAL SELLING

In addition to the above, an author should learn how to talk about their work to others. Random people. People you meet at the coffee shop. Your dentist when they don't have their hands in your mouth up to their elbows. That cousin you just started chatting with again after ten years. I mention that I've been writing, and if they indicate interest, I describe my books.

I keep a handful of business cards on me at all times, with my website, to give away to people. I know I've made sales this way. Word of mouth can be incredibly powerful, and readers love to know they've actually met an author whose work they enjoy.

I am well aware that it can be very difficult for an introverted author type to get used to promoting themselves. I know not all authors are introverted, but we tend to be, as the reclusive lifestyle of an author does match well with that of an introvert. However, if you wish your books to sell well, it's worth it to break out of your shell and talk about your book.

I took a class on "personal selling" in college as part of my accounting degree. I am half extrovert/half introvert, and I can usually emulate either side, but this was a difficult class for me. It involved sitting face-to-face with another person and praising myself, which was incredibly difficult. The class was an abject lesson in everything Imposter Syndrome told me to never do. However, I learned some tricks in the course, and will pass those on to you.

- Pretend you're talking about your favorite author. Gush about the work, the aspects you enjoy the most, be that world-building, character dialogue, or plot twists.
- Frame this as a job interview. Most of us have had to deal with those, and they really are just personal selling. Now you're in a job interview with a potential reader, selling your own talents so they will hire you.
- Work up set phrases you can use without thinking about them, like a sales patter. Some call this an "elevator pitch" for your work. This is the 10-second information

byte you might pitch to a publisher if you're stuck on an elevator with them. "I write historical fantasy, mostly set in Ireland, with a wee bit of fairy magic."
- Create some follow up lines, as well, so that's not the only response you have in your repertoire. If someone asks which of your books is your favorite, have one ready. That's a more common question than you think. It might not be one that's already published – in fact, that creates buzz for an upcoming book.

With these tricks, and some practice, you can become adept (or at least not terrified) at personal selling of your work. It takes some time to build upon the confidence, fake or otherwise, but it can help to reduce the anxiety at bragging about yourself that most of us dread.

WRITING CONTESTS

Writing contests are juried competitions where you, as the author, can enter your work and compete for a prize. The contest may be curated by:
- Form, such as short story, novel, poem, first chapter
- Genre, such as science fiction, romance, or historical fiction
- Demographic of author, such as Young Authors, students, female authors, native authors, LGBTQ+ authors
- Location of author, such as southwest America, NYC, International, rural
- Experience of author, such as unpublished, emerging

- Other criteria are always possible

There is usually a prize. Sometimes there is money, sometimes publication, sometimes just bragging rights (put it on your writing resume, though!)

> Some contests request an entry fee/reading fee,
> and some are free to enter.
> Keep in mind the entry fee is a barrier that
> limits your competition.

Pros of entering contests:

- Recognition – prizes can get you noticed, and you can put the prize on your resume or CV. If a particular book wins a prize, you can include that data on the cover and marketing material. (i.e., Winner of the Writer's Digest Short Fiction Contest, 2019)
- Motivation – contests can impel you to finish your project by a deadline
- Competition – some people thrive on trying to get better as compared to other people
- Quicker turnaround – most contests have a shorter turnaround time than publishers, so you can get feedback more quickly
- Flexibility – there are LOTS of contests out there for all sorts of genres and forms

- Opportunity – sometimes judges are also agents

Cons of entering contests:

- No payment unless you win (IF there is a cash prize and they are legit)
- Some contests have a fee to enter
- Some authors do not respond well to competition element
- Lack of theme or direction can be paralyzing
- The majority of contests give no feedback (a few do, with some listed below)

Which ones to enter?

There is a "grading" criteria I've seen on the ALLI site (Alliance of Independent Authors) that helps curate which contests are legit and which are little more than money grabs. While not EVERY contest is listed here, they mention their criteria so you can judge for yourself.

https://selfpublishingadvice.org/author-awards-contests-rated-reviewed/

(From the above website:)
1. The event exists to recognize talent, not to enrich the organizers.
- Avoid events which are driven by excessive entry fees, marketing services to entrants, or selling merchandise like stickers and certificates.

2. Receiving an award is a significant achievement.
- An event that hands out awards like Halloween candy dilutes the value of those awards, rendering them meaningless. Beware events that offer awards in dozens of categories. These are often schemes to maximize the number of winners in order to sell them stickers and other merchandise.

3. The judging process is transparent and clear.
- Watch out for contests who's judging criteria and personnel are vague or undisclosed.

4. Prizes are appropriate and commensurate with the entry fees collected.
- If a cash prize is offered, it should align with the size of the entry fee. "Exposure" is not an appropriate prize. Representation or publication are acceptable prizes, but only if offered by a reputable company without hidden fees.

5. Entrants are not required to forfeit key rights to their work.
- Avoid contests with onerous terms, especially those which require the forfeiture of publishing rights without a termination clause. When in doubt, have an independent professional review the terms.

Some other items to look for:
- "Testimonials" from unknown authors. If the contest is real, it will say something specific, such as "Last year's winner is now represented by the XX agency" which is a verifiable datum.
- High fees (over $30), especially if it's new. You have no idea on a new contest if they will even award their prize.

- Everyone who enters "wins" the prize of being in an anthology – which will cost you $60 to get your copy of. This is a form of vanity-publishing.
- Any contest that wants your exclusive or long-term rights unless they're paying you good money for those rights. Even then, be cautious. Six months to a year is reasonable for a journal. Anything longer than that, you might want to reconsider.

> **CONTEST EXERCISE:** List five free contests you would like to enter that fit your genre. List five paid contests you would like to enter that fit your genre.

CHRISTY NICHOLAS

CONCLUSION

Writing doesn't have to be frightening and wild, full of chaos and luck. You can take your passion and determination and form a plan to create what you want to create. It may take a bit of trial and error, searching for the plan that works best for you, the one that makes the most of your own talents and motivations, but there is one out there.

You don't have to be 100% planner to be a writer. You don't have to be 100% pantser. We all exist and work best on a spectrum and finding the process that works best for you can take a while. Have faith, keep trying new ways, and eventually you'll settle on a system that works best with your motivations, determination, inspiration, and time schedule. Yes, even if you are a stay-at-home mom who home schools five children. I know, an author friend of mine does exactly that! She gets up at 4:30am to get time to write without children.

Each of us work in a different way, but if you work up a plan, it just might help you craft a tighter story, spend less time writing it, and more time enjoying it.

Remember, no one is born a planner. We aren't born pantsers, either. In fact, we're born without plans OR pants!

We work on the steps, we learn the tricks, and we become the Extreme Planner we want in our lives. It's a process, and one that you, too, can excel at, if you want to.

Read the final product of the example used in this book! Check out *Misfortune of Vision,* the fourth book in The Druid's Brooch Series

A magical gift of the fae. When a soothsayer faces her end of days, can she find her lone heir before more blood is spilled?

Buy *Misfortune of Vision* to match wits with fate today!

books2read.com/Misfortune-of-Vision

THANK YOU!

Thank you so much for enjoying Extreme Planning for Authors. If you've enjoyed the book, please consider leaving a review to help others find this resource.

Giving a review to an author is like the applause at the end of a concert, and authors greatly appreciate them!

If you would like to get updates, sneak previews, FREE STUFF, and contests, please sign up for my newsletter.

www.GreenDragonArtist.com

OTHER BOOKS BY THIS AUTHOR

See all the books available through Green Dragon Publishing at

www.GreenDragonArtist.com/Books

RESOURCES

- The Snowflake Method: https://www.advancedfictionwriting.com/articles/snowflake-method/
- AgentQuery.com – a place to search for an agent who might be interested in your genre
- Examples of successful queries: http://agentqueryconnect.com/index.php?/forum/25-aq-connect-examples-of-successful-queries/
- http://www.guidetoliteraryagents.com/blog/CategoryView,category,SuccessfulQueries.aspx
- Query Shark: http://queryshark.blogspot.com/
- Query Critique Corner: http://agentqueryconnect.com/index.php?/forum/2-aq-connect-query-critiques/
- http://www.writersdigest.com/editor-blogs/guide-to-literary-agents/successful-queries
- Pet Peeves of Agents: http://www.writersdigest.com/editor-blogs/guide-to-literary-agents/pubtips-pet-peeves
- A professional agent critique of a query letter, point by point: http://www.writersdigest.com/online-editor/how-to-write-the-perfect-query-letter
- http://www.writersdigest.com/editor-blogs/guide-to-literary-agents/successful-queries/brianna-shrum-querying-choosing-literary-agent
- Absolute Write Water Cooler – has a forum to critique queries and ask about particular agents. https://absolutewrite.com/forums
- Contest sites to check: Writers Beware, Alli, and other watchdog sites.
- https://www.sfwa.org/other-resources/for-authors/writer-beware/

- https://selfpublishingadvice.org/author-awards-contests-rated-reviewed/
- https://winningwriters.com/the-best-free-literary-contests/contests-to-avoid
- https://www.victoriastrauss.com/advice/contests/
- https://www.writing-world.com/contests/scams.shtml

ABOUT THE AUTHOR

Christy Nicholas writes under several pen names, including Emeline Rhys, CN Jackson, and Rowan Dillon. She is an author, artist, and accountant. After she failed to become an airline pilot, she quit her ceaseless pursuit of careers that begin with the letter 'A' and decided to concentrate on her writing. Since she has Project Completion Compulsion, she is one of the few authors with no unfinished novels.

Christy has her hands in many crafts, including digital art, beaded jewelry, writing, and photography. In real life, she's a CPA, but having grown up with art all around her (her mother, grandmother, and great-grandmother are/were all artists), it sort of infected her, as it were.

She wants to expose the incredible beauty in this world, hidden beneath the everyday grime of familiarity and habit, and share it with others. She uses characters out of time and places infused with magic and myth, writing magical realism stories in both historical fantasy and time travel flavors.

Website: www.greendragonartist.com
Blog: www.greendragonartist.net
www.facebook.com/greendragonauthor
www.bookbub.com/profile/christy-nicholas
www.instagram.com/greendragonartist9

www.ingramcontent.com/pod-product-compliance
Lightning Source LLC
Chambersburg PA
CBHW032031290426
44110CB00012B/758